Growing Whole

Self-Realization on an Endangered Planet

Molly Young Brown

Hazelden Educational Materials
Center City, Minnesota 55012-0176

ISBN: 0-89486-865-9

Library of Congress Cataloging-in-Publication Data
Brown, Molly Young.
    Growing whole : self-realization on an endangered planet / Molly Young Brown.
        p.   cm.
    Includes bibliographical references and index.
    1. Psychosynthesis. I. Title.
RC489.P76B76 1993
158.9—dc20   92-34687
                                                                         CIP

Editor's note
    Hazelden Educational Materials offers a variety of information on chemical depen-
dency and related areas. Our publications do not necessarily represent Hazelden's
programs, nor do they officially speak for any Twelve Step organization.

The following publishers and authors have given permission to use extended quota-
tions from these copyrighted works:

Reprinted from *The Plum Village Chanting Book,* Parallax Press, Berkeley, CA, 1991.

From *Holy The Firm,* by Annie Dillard. Copyright 1977 by Annie Dillard. Reprinted by
    permission of HarperCollins Publishers.

From *Psychosynthesis,* by Roberto Assagioli. Copyright 1976 by Berkshire Center for
    Psychosynthesis.

From *The Act to Will,* by Roberto Assagioli. Copyright 1974 by Berkshire Center for
    Psychosynthesis.

From *Disturbing the Peace,* by Vaclav Havel. Copyright 1990 by HarperCollins
    Publishers.

From *What We May Be,* by Piero Ferrucci. Copyright 1982 by Piero Ferrucci.
    Reprinted by permission of Piero Ferrucci.

From *Roots of Buddhist Psychology,* by Jack Kornfield. Reprinted by permission of Jack
    Kornfield.

About the author

    Molly Young Brown, M.A., has worked in psychosynthesis as a counselor
and trainer for more than twenty years. In 1973 she and her husband, Jim,
studied with founder Roberto Assagioli in Italy. Molly is the author of *The
Unfolding Self: Psychosynthesis and Counseling* (1983) as well as articles on
psychosynthesis, peace psychology, and deep ecology. She has conducted
training programs and workshops across the United States, in Canada, and
in the former Soviet Union.

Contents

Planetary crises require a transformation in our thinking and values. What is psychosynthesis? Suggestions on using this book: maps and models, exercises, drawing, familiar territory.

What is self-awareness? Checking in: feelings, thoughts, attitudes, body sensations. Who is aware? Developing an Observer. The evening review.

Where am I now in my life? Keeping a journal. Free drawing. Dreaming. Your autobiography. Accepting where we are now.

Identification and disidentification. What is Self? Letter to Self. Meditation. Presence. The Perfect Companion.

Levels of consciousness. The "egg" diagram. The repression of the sublime. Opening the door to the superconscious. The Wise Being.

What is possible for me now in my life? Exploring purpose. An ideal model.

What's getting in my way? Subpersonalities: the many faces of everyone. Seeking a loyal soldier. Journey to the Wise Being.

To Jim:
my soul mate,
life partner,
and best friend

Foreword by Jacquelyn Small

OUR WORLD IS IN A SPIRITUAL CRISIS. This means, of course, that most human beings are as well. Psychology is having to expand because human beings are. What is needed today, more than anything, is a new vision and hope for a future we can all co-create—a future representative of who we truly are as human souls. For this hope to manifest, however, we are in dire need of a model and philosophy of the Self that includes all of who we are, a model of *wholeness*. When our entire human nature is taken into account, we begin to recognize that *we are not human beings learning to be spiritual; we are spiritual beings learning to be human!*

Most psychological theories are based on philosophies that focus only on the past—our fragmentation, neuroses, and disease. Principles of *wholeness* (from the root word *hal,* which also means "health" and "holy") are rarely taught. And the ways to discover our whole and true nature are seldom even considered when we seek out professionals for help. Today, psychology is being challenged to catch up with our rapidly unfolding spiritual nature, and Molly Brown's work in psychosynthesis offers us a way. This book is representative of this wholistic psychospiritual approach.

The one thing I've learned in my twenty-four years of "people-helping" is this: When people begin to heal the wounds of their past and learn to take full responsibility for their lives, they discover they are naturally good, truthful, and already have a built-in loving concern for others and the world we all share. In other words, behind all our suffering and dysfunction there already resides a being who is divine, a soul who is both willing and able to be fully conscious as a human being. In the midst of so much crisis and the fragmented teachings about the Self, we've lost our way. True helpers are those who can lead us once more to our inner healer. Today, a psychospiritual approach to healing is what we require to pull ourselves up and out of our distress, so we can progress to our next right step, which is the acknowledgment and unfolding of our wholistic human/spiritual nature.

When we work from a model of the Self that is based in wholeness, taking into account all our motivations, both lowly and high, our various levels of consciousness, and our spiritual powers as a human soul, we feel "at home." We feel complete. In my work with thousands of people in recovery, I've found that the healing of our emotional wounds happens when people can strengthen their inner connection with a Higher Self and a God of their understanding. But we cannot simply jump over our past hurts, either, or attempt to by-pass the psychological and interpersonal work needed to be "spiritual." Healing happens in two ways: we must go backward and focus on our wounds so they can heal, while steadily moving forward toward higher and more integrated identities. Both our personal and transpersonal selves must be recognized and addressed if we are to experience wholeness.

Molly Young Brown's first book, *The Unfolding Self,* has been carried by our counselor training institute now for nearly ten years. Her book is extremely popular, as I know *Growing*

Whole will be. Molly is a wonderful teacher in helping us all learn practical ways to access our inner healers and draw out the potential buried within ourselves. There is a saying in the counseling field, coined by Ram Dass, that "therapy is as high as the therapist." So whether you are one who helps others or one seeking help, *Growing Whole* will expand you and those you serve.

In this book, you will discover for yourself the simplicity and bountifulness of the Self as it turns toward health and wholeness, responding with loving action to our ailing planet's needs. You won't stop with just working on your personal self; you will develop your transpersonal Self as well. You will discover on every page ways that will lead you back through your past and on to an identity with your highest nature, the Higher Self.

The process of psychosynthesis, on which principles this book is founded, takes you through a personal, an interpersonal, and ultimately a transpersonal synthesis of all your fragmented "parts." You then arrive at your station of wholeness in the end. You will discover that everything about yourself that you need to know, love, and understand can be contained within the boundaries of this philosophy. Molly's guidance is simple and direct, though based in the highest metaphysical truth. Anyone who is interested in this book will easily understand it. This is what I love about Molly's way of teaching.

Dr. Roberto Assagioli, who developed psychosynthesis, was an Italian psychiatrist who died in 1974. At one time, he was a student of Sigmund Freud. I wish I'd had the privilege of knowing him personally as Molly did because I know he was an advanced human being and master teacher. His philosophy greatly influences my own work and books. One of the first stories I heard about Dr. Assagioli not only warmed my heart, but captured the nature of the journey you are about to take while studying and participating in the process of *Growing Whole*.

One day Dr. Freud called Dr. Assagioli in Italy and asked him to consider introducing psychoanalysis to the Italian medical community. Dr. Assagioli replied (and I paraphrase): "Well, Dr. Freud, I would be delighted to. However, you must know that I will have to make some adjustments in your theories if I am to teach them. You see, you teach that we are a house with a basement and a first floor; while, in my theoretical house, there is a basement, a first floor, a second floor, a third floor, a sun roof, and an elevator."

It is my pleasure to introduce you to Molly Brown and her writings on *Growing Whole*. May your journey through this clearly written and dynamic book lead you to the sun roof of your life.

In love,
Jacquelyn Small

Acknowledgments

MY GRATITUDE AND APPRECIATION GO OUT TO THE FOLLOWING:

Rebecca Post, my editor, who has worked so supportively and cooperatively to help give birth to the book of my dreams.

Ling Lucas, my agent, whose feedback and perseverance improved the book and found it the perfect publishing home.

John Firman, for fine-tuning the concepts, especially on the nature of Self.

Walter Polt, for his invaluable contribution to the section on anger.

Jacqueline Small, for her enthusiastic belief in my work, and her sparkling foreword.

John and Emma Lou Young, my parents, for feedback on the early chapters and their unflagging love and support.

Bob Kimball, for feedback on the final chapters and for helping me see and clarify deeper currents.

Gary and Francine Foltz, for their longtime friendship and for helping me choose the title.

Remis Bistrickas of Lithuania, who as much as ordered me to write this book in 1989.

Jim, Gregory, Cassidy, and my sister *Judy,* for growing whole together with me all these years and always cheering me on.

Introduction: Seeking a Path

*O*URS IS A TIME OF PERIL AND TRANSFORMATION. In the last few years, we have seen unparalleled political change with the breakup of the Communist world and the end of the Cold War. Eastern European peoples regained control of their governments, the infamous Berlin Wall was demolished, and the Soviet Union dissolved. This transformation, however, was marked in many of the former Soviet republics by an intensification of the often bloody struggles for ethnic identity and independence, and by severe economic crisis and hardship.

The end of the Cold War lessened fears of nuclear holocaust but has made little difference in the level of peace on the planet. Military build-up, the sale of arms, and armed conflicts continue around the globe, involving innocent civilians in the power struggles of the mighty. Many of the victims of this warfare are already struggling to survive in the midst of oppression and poverty.

During this time, the United States was involved in controversial military actions in Central America and the Persian Gulf, while at home savings and loan institutions, banks, and insurance companies collapsed from mismanagement and shady deals. More and more homeless appeared on the streets, the national debt soared, the economy soured, and urban unrest dramatically increased. In the United States and around the world, our political and economic systems seem unable to cope with human realities at the end of the twentieth century.

We have also seen a world-wide awakening of concern for the planetary environment. In the United States, the twentieth anniversary of Earth Day captured the attention of the mainstream, while recycling and energy conservation became household words and practices. Young people especially have taken up the cause of defending the environment from destruction.

Nevertheless, we continue to hear of the devastation of the rain forests, damage to the ozone layer, loss of arable land to desertification, the accumulation and accidental spilling of radioactive and other toxic wastes, the destruction of ancient ecosystems, the extinction of thousands of species. We can no longer deny that our life support systems on planet Earth are gravely imperiled, perhaps beyond repair.

How do we find our way in such a world? Thinkers and writers concerned with the future of the planet all speak of the need for change in thinking, in attitude, in cultural values, beginning with the individual. What is the nature of this change and how will it occur? How can we help awaken our human potential and put it to work to support peace, justice, and environmental health in the world?

Many of us yearn to make a difference, to make it better for ourselves, for each other, and for our children. We want to understand ourselves and this multidimensional world in which we live. We sense we must learn and grow as individuals at the same time as we try to change things around us. We want to become more effective and more healing in our actions. We want to feel connected with the natural world around us and with each other. We seek wisdom and wholeness.

There are many paths, many truths, many teachings, that can guide us in our search. Through this self-study book, I offer a path that many have found powerful and harmonious. It is called *psychosynthesis* and is based on the work of Italian psychiatrist Roberto Assagioli (1888-1974) and many others inspired by him. I have studied, taught, and counseled with this approach for twenty years and have used its perspectives and tools in my own growth throughout those years.

Psychosynthesis is an intimidating word to many people. Even those of us who have worked with this approach for many years often wish Assagioli had chosen a different name for it. If we break it down to root words, however, the meaning becomes clearer. Just as "psycho-analysis" means the analysis of the psyche, "psycho-synthesis" means the synthesis of the psyche. Psychoanalysis seeks to understand human psychology by exploring the various components of the psyche. Psychosynthesis seeks to bring these components together in a unified, integrated whole so each person can respond creatively and joyfully to the psychological and spiritual demands of life.

Psychosynthesis draws upon many traditions. It incorporates many principles and practices from Buddhism, yoga, and other Eastern philosophies, as well as from Western spiritual traditions, philosophy, and psychology. For many people in the West, psychosynthesis offers a comfortable bridge into the wisdom of the East. As I study Buddhism in more depth, I find so much that is familiar to me from my years of work in psychosynthesis. I seem to have already learned the basics!

The psychosynthesis approach is uniquely suited to our time. It recognizes the many dimensions of our concerns and our potentials: physical, emotional, mental, interpersonal, social, and spiritual. It coaches each person in seeking his or her unique inner truth and way in harmony with the needs

and forces of nature. It offers basic, flexible models and principles for understanding and integrating all the parts of ourselves. It offers a wide variety of tools for discovery and
choice.

Most important, psychosynthesis helps us bring our gifts
into action in the world. Our families and communities, local to
global, are enriched and healed as we learn about ourselves
and our astonishing potentials, and as we act from that self-
knowledge. We discover, inevitably, that we are not separate
from each other nor from the Earth which sustains us. We
realize our interdependence with all life on Earth. We learn to
act from the "Ecological Self," a term coined by
philosopher/ecologist Arne Naess. We grow whole, together.

I hope *Growing Whole* will accompany you on your journey
toward wholeness, toward becoming who you most deeply
are. I welcome your companionship on this journey that we all
share as we struggle together to awaken from the confusion,
denial, fear, and violence that surround us in the world today.
Together we are already moving to redeem ourselves and our
planetary home for future generations, for a common life of
peace, beauty, love, and joy. I promise you the process will
hold more than struggle for us; we will also know laughter,
surprise, adventure, and deep satisfaction.

SUGGESTIONS ON USING THIS BOOK

In the following pages, you will find perspectives, principles,
and models to stimulate your understanding and exercises for
experimenting with the processes. I recommend that you keep
a journal for recording your responses to the text and to the
exercises as you go along. Certainly the exercises will be of
greatest benefit if you take the time to go through them,

reflect on your experience, and make the notes and drawings suggested in each one.

If you choose to read front to back, you will follow my sense of a logical order, working from awareness of the present, through visions for the future, to confronting the blocks to your paths and choosing the changes you need. The final chapters speak to the special challenges of spiritual awakening, relationships, and service in the world. You may also choose to dip into topics of particular interest to you, reading other parts later. Many later sections refer to previous exercises that are related to the issue or process under discussion. This may give you some guidance in following your own order of study.

Maps and Models

Many of us need some conceptual models to understand our experience and to learn new attitudes and perspectives. The models serve as symbols for various attitudes and help remind us of what is possible, what we are reaching for. They represent our understanding of our psychological process at the time we use them, but they do not represent the ultimate truth about our psyches. Like maps of a territory we plan to explore, our conceptual models are representations drawn from individual experience, measurements, observations, and estimations. But maps are not the territory, and models are not our psyches. When our experience and needs depart from the model, we need to either revise the model or discard it.

Psychosynthesis theory has developed many models and maps that will be offered at appropriate points in the book. We will discuss the Observer, subpersonalities, the "egg diagram," and several other useful conceptualizations of the human psyche. Try these models on for size, explore your inner world through their lenses, and give them an opportunity to enrich your understanding. Then, in the end, revise them or discard them according to your own needs and your own wisdom.

Exercises

Because this is a self-study book, the exercises are designed to be used as you come to them. However, some people prefer to get an overview of a whole section by skimming through a chapter before actually doing the reflecting and writing. Work whichever way is best for you. You may find it best to skip over the exercises until you are ready to actually go through them, so that your rational/logical mind doesn't pre-program your responses.

Above all, trust yourself and your own way of working. I like to think of psychosynthesis as a moveable jungle gym that people can climb on in any way they wish. The jungle gym responds gently to your movements, so that you affect its shape and configuration while it provides a flexible structure for your exercise. I hope this book can work that way for you, too.

The exercises come from a variety of sources, many difficult to trace. There is something of an oral tradition in psychosynthesis, in which people share ideas and techniques in workshops and seminars without necessarily stating where the ideas originated. Whenever possible, I will mention the origins of exercises, or note that "this exercise synthesizes ideas and techniques from many sources." Exercises without such notations have been developed especially for this book out of my experience of this rich tradition.

Drawing

When we write responses to questions, we usually call upon our conscious, rational mind. Drawing is a way of tapping the unconscious, which tends to communicate to us in the form of images, sounds, sensations, or other nonverbal sensory impressions. Words may accompany these messages from the unconscious, but they tend to be direct and to-the-point, rather than the more lengthy explanations of the rational mind.

Many of the exercises ask you to make a drawing in response to a question or meditative process. The problem is that many of us feel very inadequate about drawing, perhaps because of early childhood experiences with critical teachers or adults. Most of us have little artistic talent or have not discovered what we have. Nevertheless, it is very important to our wholeness that we reclaim our artistic rights. Skill at drawing is no more important than needing voice lessons to sing in the shower. We can use stick figures and simple symbols, and still express something beyond words. So I invite you to take some risks and use those crayons! You can always keep your drawings private until you feel comfortable sharing them with others.

Familiar Territory

Readers who have worked with other approaches to personal and spiritual growth may find much that is familiar here. Many of the concepts, principles, and methods are shared with other teachings. Assagioli and his successors have all brought wisdom from other traditions they have studied and practiced, Eastern and Western. Various traditions and paths, including psychosynthesis, seek to discover and articulate universal principles of human growth, and often arrive at similar conclusions.

When you find yourself in familiar territory, relax and enjoy the validation of what you already know. You may choose to skim through these sections or use them for review of basic understandings. (There is always more depth and subtlety to discover in these simple processes.) I hope you will find new perspectives on familiar territories, as well as brand-new regions for exploration. No doubt you will have some insights of your own to add to what appears here. Many paths, many traditions, and all our collective wisdom are needed to bring the human potential to full flower as a sustaining part of the life of the Earth.

1. Self-Awareness: The First Step

WHO AM I? What is my part to play in the world? What am I here for? What am I supposed to be doing? Can I do anything to really change things?

Questions like these may lie in our hearts unanswered for many years while we go about the business of daily life and personal survival. Sooner or later, however, they rise to the surface, often to our great discomfort. As we see the world in turmoil and peril around us, we wonder how we can possibly make a difference. If we don't know who we are, how can we be anything but cogs in the Machine, or extras in the crowd scenes?

How we can make a difference is inextricably linked to who we are. And to discover that, we begin by practicing self-awareness, right now, in this moment. This is the first step in our journey toward wholeness.

Awareness is the essential ingredient in any process of growth. Without awareness, we can act only out of conditioning and habit. So let's begin with a simple awareness practice, noticing how we experience our bodies, our feelings, our thoughts, and our environment.

⚭

Checking In

Close your eyes and sit quietly in a comfortable position.

As you do so, begin to notice any sensations in your body.

Notice any areas of tension or discomfort.

What is happening in your shoulders? Your jaw? Your thighs? Your belly? . . .

Notice your breathing.

Notice sounds you can hear around you.

Notice the feel of the air against your skin, its relative warmth or coolness.

Notice how the ground feels beneath you, how your chair and the floor support your weight.

Look around you for a moment, and see what you see. . . .

Now notice any feelings about your body or about what you have noticed so far. Do you feel annoyed or surprised? Do you feel excited or anxious? Do you feel just kind of neutral? Or perhaps you are not sure what you feel. . . .

Notice any feelings that seem to be in response to the world around you. Notice feelings that seem to come entirely from "inside. . . ."

Now let your attention focus on your thoughts.

Even while you read these words, other thoughts may be going on in the background of your mind or in response to what you read.

Notice any insights or concepts you have about this process.

Notice any judgements, pro or con.

Notice questions and concerns. Notice images. . . .

Observe for a moment how easy or difficult this seems to be for you. Do you find it easier to observe one aspect than another? Is it possible to distinguish between feelings and thoughts, or between feelings and body sensations? . . .

Make some notes about your experience in your journal.

⚭

WHAT DOES IT MEAN?

The first question to arise at this point may be, *What is the meaning of what I observe?* Most of us find it difficult to simply observe ourselves in this way, without immediately passing judgement, interpreting, or deciding to change what we observe. That tendency may be a factor in our inability to be aware. We fear awareness because of the demands or expectations that are usually attached. Why would I want to notice tension in my shoulders if it just means I am doing something wrong or that I may have some disease process going on? Why would I want to feel my feelings if they are labeled "crazy" or "inappropriate"? So our first task may be to learn to observe without making any judgement or analysis—not an easy undertaking!

Observing with Detachment

We can begin by simply observing the judgements, analyses, or expectations. "Oh, now I am judging those feelings. . . . Now I am thinking about what I should do about my tight shoulders. . . . Now I am trying to figure out why I feel this way." As soon as we observe a process, we step away from it; we detach somewhat from that perspective. We become more of a neutral Observer of all that is going on within.

UNCOMFORTABLE FEELINGS

Another difficulty arises when I notice what I am feeling and I don't like it. I feel depression and pain, or anger. Isn't it better to just ignore such feelings and go on about my business instead of paying attention to them and maybe making them worse?

The problem is that feelings we ignore still affect us. They sink beneath the level of our awareness and nibble away at our well-being. They pop out at inappropriate times or get dumped on people we don't really want to hurt. Or they may lower our levels of energy and joy so that we operate out of a narrow band of blandness and mediocrity.

Respect the Feelings

Noticing feelings does not necessarily mean plunging into them, although on occasion we might choose to do so. Noticing feelings does mean giving them respectful attention, being ready to learn from them about ourselves or our situation. If I notice that I am feeling depressed, I can take a look at what might be provoking my depression. Maybe I am neglecting my basic needs in some way. Maybe my communication with my spouse is off the track, so we are not really connecting. Maybe an old wound has opened up and is ready now to drain and heal if given some attention. Maybe something is wrong in my environment—a gas leak or an increase in air or noise pollution. Maybe I am unconsciously picking up subtle conflicts in my family or at work. Maybe I am anxious about something I half heard on the news, such as threats of a new war or environmental disaster. If I ignore my feelings of depression, I may suffer unnecessarily and overlook early signs of a developing problem. I may carry my anxiety inside, instead of bringing it outside where I can possibly address its causes.

Feel the Feelings

Sometimes it is important to just feel the hard feelings, to go into them and through them. Feelings are natural and may guide us through a necessary process of change. When we are grieving over a loss, for example, we need to feel our feelings, express them, trust them, and follow them through to a place of acceptance and peace. Similarly, allowing ourselves to go through anger in a safe setting will often put us in touch with our deepest values, giving us a sense of commitment and power. Joanna Macy, in her "Despair and Empowerment" workshops, has helped many people acknowledge and work through their feelings of despair about what is happening to the planet. This is so they may discover within themselves a creative force for change. In this book, chapter 7, "Transforming the Demons Within," explores how we can work with the so-called negative feelings of anger, grief, and fear.

The next exercise will help you to direct, expand, and focus your awareness in various ways while you sense the "source" of your awareness within.[1]

∞

Who Is Aware?

Close your eyes and take a few minutes to simply breathe and quiet yourself. Allow your shoulders and jaw to loosen and relax. . . .

Now notice your breathing. Notice how the air feels as it enters your nose, flows down your windpipe, and into your lungs. Notice how the muscles of your chest and belly respond to the in-breath and the out-breath. . . .

Allow your awareness to enlarge to include the whole trunk of your body, back, sides, shoulders, and pelvic area. . . .

Now include your head and face, your arms and hands, your legs and feet. Is it possible to be aware of your whole body, all at once?

Ask yourself: Who is aware of this body? . . .

Now notice whatever feelings and emotions are present right now. Notice feelings that have come up during this exercise. Notice feelings that have been carried over from before. . . .

Notice your thoughts and your thinking process. Watch the images, words, impressions, judgements, insights, chatter. . . .

Ask yourself: Who is aware of these feelings and thoughts? . . .

Now allow your awareness to expand to include the room in which you are sitting. Feel the temperature and quality of the air. . . . Listen to the sounds. . . . Open your eyes for a few moments and look around you. . . .

Allow your awareness to include the whole house around you . . . and then the surrounding area. . . . Perhaps you can hear birds singing outside, or dogs barking. . . . Imagine that you can be aware of the life going on in the surrounding area, beyond what you can directly see, hear, and touch. . . .

Continue expanding your field of awareness now to include the entire region where you are located. In your mind, touch the houses and office buildings, the forests, lakes, and streams, the streets and highways, the people, plants, and animals, the geological formations. . . .

Ask yourself: Who is aware? . . .

Include now the whole continent in your awareness. Imagine you can silently touch all the people on this continent as they go about their lives. . . . Include specific friends and relatives in this awareness. . . .

As you embrace the whole continent with your awareness, what do you see and hear? What do you feel? What are you aware of? . . .

Now expand your awareness even more to encompass the whole hemisphere . . . and then the whole planet. . . . Allow yourself to be aware of the beauty and the suffering of the whole planet, and of all its living beings. . . . Be aware of the planet floating in space, making its journey around the sun. . . .

Take some time with this. . . .

Now be aware of your breath, in and out. . . . Be aware of any body sensations, feelings, and thoughts. . . .

Ask yourself: Who is aware? Who is aware of the whole planet in one moment and aware of simply breathing in the next? Who is aware? . . .

When you feel ready, make some notes in your journal about your experience, both what you were aware of and what you sensed in response to the question "Who is aware?"

∞

The question "Who is aware?" represents one of the most persistent challenges of philosophy. How can we be aware of being aware? How can we observe ourselves observing? In a way, we can never answer the question, at least not with definite words and concepts. We can only explore our inner responses to the question, responses beyond words and definitions. We can only rely on our individual experience to lead us to some sense of deep knowing of who it is who is aware.

DEVELOPING AN OBSERVER

When I am aware of my body sensations, my feelings, my thoughts, and the world around me, I experience myself as an Observer, calmly and compassionately watching and listening, inside and out. It may seem like begging the question to speak of the Observer as the one who is aware. I find it helpful, however, because much of the time I am not particularly aware; I am identified instead with passing feelings, thoughts, and physical states. My Observer is an identification I can assume when I want to be more aware of myself and of what is going on around me. The Observer symbolizes the attitude of nonjudgemental awareness I am cultivating; this symbol can help me move into such an attitude when I am confused or distracted.

Looking from Outside

I recall a time when my children were very small and my husband and I were living in a mobile home on the Stanford University campus while he attended a summer school program. There was no air-conditioning in the mobile home, and it had very poor ventilation. I was in an unfamiliar setting, knew few people in the area, and was generally having a hard time. One day I was particularly despairing, dealing with some intestinal disturbance on top of everything else. I found myself looking at myself as if from the outside, and from above. I described myself in the third person: "Here's Molly, feeling very lonely and sick." I felt a tremendous surge of compassion for myself, as I might have felt toward one of my children in such a circumstance. It was a powerful and healing moment, and as the sick and lonely person, I immediately felt relief. This was a powerful experience of becoming an Observer of my experience, rather than only being caught up in it.

∽

Developing an Observer

What qualities do you imagine an Observer would have? What images come to mind when you think about the idea of an Observer? . . . How would you like an Observer to appear? Consider facial expression, body posture, dress, age, and gender. . . .

When you have a positive, comfortable image, imagine being the Observer and see how it feels. . . .

If you need to make some changes now that you are the Observer, do so. . . . Then take some time to get used to being the Observer, so you can recall the experience later and return to it when needed. For a few minutes, observe your body sensations, feelings, and thoughts, as well as the world around you from this perspective. . . .

In your journal, you may want to describe your Observer in words or create a drawing to represent the qualities of your Observer.

∽

A Bigger Container

The American Zen master Charlotte Joko Beck writes in *Everyday Zen* about the usefulness of creating "A Bigger Container" for our feelings and thoughts, especially troublesome ones: "What is created, what grows, is the amount of life I can hold without it upsetting me, dominating me."[2] It seems to me that our Observer is just that: a bigger container to hold more and more life, without becoming lost in particular feelings or thoughts. We still have our feelings! But no single feeling can control us for long. And this is of vital importance when we become aware of the anguish and despair that many of us feel in response to the suffering and destruction all around us and all around the Earth.

Self-awareness takes practice. The following method that can be used daily to develop the Observer and deepen nonjudgemental self-awareness is called the Evening Review.[3]

∽

The Evening Review

This exercise is best done at the end of your day. Just before going to sleep, review your day in your mind, playing it back like a movie, only backward. Begin with where you are right now, then recall the events of the late evening, then the time of early evening, dinnertime, the afternoon, and so on until the morning when you awoke. Recall how the events felt to you, how you responded in feelings and thought as well as overt action.

You may use this review to examine yourself and your life as a whole, without judgement, or you may focus on some aspect of yourself, on some pattern you would like to know more about, on some specific inner process you may want to explore. The attitude with which you do the review is most important. When you examine your day, try to do it as a detached, nonjudgemental Observer, calmly and clearly registering each phase of what has happened. Then move on to the next phase without excitement, without becoming elated at an apparent success or depressed and down on yourself about an apparent failure or mistake. The aim is a calm registering in consciousness of the meaning and patterns of the day rather than a reliving of it.

As you review the day, you also have the opportunity to observe your immediate reactions to the review: judgements, emotions, regrets, hopes, questions, concerns. Allow these responses to register calmly as well.

This exercise may be combined with the "Checking In" exercise found earlier in this chapter. It may be useful to write down your observations, together with any insights or impressions that come, as part of your personal journal. By reviewing entries recorded over a period of time, you may observe patterns not otherwise apparent.

Ah, So!

Spiritual teacher Ram Dass often speaks of an attitude of calm acceptance exemplified by the monk who greeted each event, pleasant or unpleasant, with the gentle exclamation, "Ah, so!" I often think of that phrase when doing an evening review or observing some life event from this detached, accepting perspective: "The clutch went out on the car today. Ah, so!" "I received an invitation to speak at an important conference. Ah, so!" "I am frustrated and scared about my financial situation. Ah, so!"

Of course, this phrase could easily become a slogan for shutting down feelings and becoming numbly detached from life, but that is not the purpose. Our purpose is to allow ourselves the full range of emotions, from elation and celebration to despondency and despair. Paradoxically, this may be far more possible as we learn to maintain a calm, compassionate Observer who serves as an anchor for our emotional and mental health, an anchor for awareness of ourselves and our world. As we become more accustomed to observing our responses to our personal lives, we can more readily observe our responses to events in the larger world around us. We become more able to contain and experience the fullness of our love and anguish for our endangered planet and its peoples.

2. *Beginning Where We Are Now*

I WAKE UP ONE MORNING with a sore throat and cough. I have so much to do today, I can't afford to be sick. So I slap on a bandage: I take a decongestant and antihistamine and go on about my business, feeling lousy but able to function. Maybe I have to do this for several days until the cold finally goes away.

I can comfort myself with the thought that it worked; my cold got better even without my resting. I guess I did the right thing. But then a couple of weeks later I am still feeling tired all the time, or maybe the cold recurs. I have treated the cold at the level of symptoms; I have neither explored why I caught it to begin with nor inquired what my body and soul may really need. I have not looked at the whole of my life and the world around me. The cold was an opportunity to be aware of some of the dynamics of my life right now, a clear message that all may not be well.

This is not to say that treating the symptoms is inappropriate. We need bandages to keep the wounds clean and safe while they heal. We may need to use decongestants with a cold. But we also need to stop, look, and listen to the whole of our lives from time to time. If we make a practice of this kind of checking in with ourselves, we may not need the cold to remind us. We may become aware of our stress levels or need for rest before we become ill.

A BROAD PERSPECTIVE

We cannot hope to find solutions to problems—or even to know clearly what the problems are—without paying attention to the whole context within which the problems occur. We need a broad understanding of the scope, the quality, and the interrelationships of our current situation. When we react to a life crisis by merely putting on bandages, we can do more harm than good, because we are not taking into account the needs and dynamics of the whole person we each are.

This is true on social and global levels as well. Our environmental, economic, and political crises are extremely complex, affected by many interrelated forces and events. When we attempt to resolve them by piecemeal efforts, slapping on a bandage or a dramatic "quick fix," we usually make things worse. Successful attempts to make things better begin with an in-depth understanding of the situation, with intellectual as well as emotional awareness of the whole picture.

Relying on Our Unconscious

Can we really be aware of everything? Probably not, at least not with our conscious minds alone. We cannot hold all the information we take in every day in our immediate field of conscious awareness. Neither can we think everything through on this level. We must rely on the vast reservoir of our unconscious to store, organize, and process most of the massive amounts of information and experience of our lives.

So after observing and learning as much as we can within a reasonable amount of time, we can turn to our unconscious to offer us insights and guidance. We can tune in to the subtle cues of imagery, feelings, and hunches. We can inquire—and listen—within.

The following exercise may help you get an overview of your own life, an intuitive "reading" from your unconscious as well as your conscious mind. This is the first drawing exercise in the book, so you may need to recall the ideas suggested in the Introduction about drawing. Remember that drawing provides another avenue for your unconscious to express itself; words are often too concrete and rational to reflect the subtleties of the unconscious accurately. You do not have to be an artist to do a drawing; use stick figures and symbols or whatever you can to represent your feelings and images. This drawing is for you, and no one else. So give it a try. (This exercise synthesizes ideas and techniques from many sources.)

☙

Where Am I Now in My Life?

Use a sheet of paper or a page in your journal. Have drawing materials ready, such as oil pastels, colored markers, or crayons. Sit in a comfortable, upright position and close your eyes. Take a few moments to simply breathe and sit, allowing your body to come to rest. . . .

Now quietly observe your feelings and thoughts. Let them be there and let them also come to rest. . . .

Find a quiet place inside where you can be open, receptive, and patient; where you can receive responses from within. Allow yourself to abide in that place as you contemplate the following question. . . .

Where am I now in my life?

Allow images, sensations, feelings, and thoughts to arise in response and simply observe them. . . .

When you feel ready, find a way of capturing that response on paper—in colors, shapes, symbols, or pictures.

☙

Exploring the Drawing's Meanings

When your drawing is finished, you can explore its subtler meanings as you would a dream. (See the section on dream interpretation under the heading "Dreaming" on page 27.) What does the drawing say to you? How do you feel after doing it? Write about any feelings and thoughts you have in your journal.

You might share your drawing with a trusted friend and, in talking about it, understand more of its implications. You may want to set the drawing aside for a day or two and take a fresh look at it to notice what you may not have seen before.

I have used this exercise countless times to check in on my current state. My drawings always reveal some facet of my life that had been out of my awareness before. Various ones have hung on the wall of my bedroom or study for months on end. Sometimes when I go to take one down, I find I am not finished absorbing its message. So it stays up a little longer. Then there comes a time when I know I have moved on, and I can file the drawing with my old journals, or even throw it away without a qualm. By then another has usually come to take its place.

Seeing Alternatives

As we attend to our present reality, we begin to experience a sense of greater choice as the vistas of our personal and social landscapes open before us. We begin to see alternatives we missed when we were constricted to a narrower field of feeling, thought, and identity. As we become aware of a new alternative, however, it is tempting to grab hold of it, constricting ourselves once again to a partial picture of what is. To further complicate things, acting on the new alternatives changes the very nature of our reality, opening yet more vistas and possibilities while leaving others behind.

So if we check in only occasionally on our present reality, we limit our options and perspective. We need ongoing inner work and specific practices to help us focus our awareness on where we are now . . . and now . . . and now.

KEEPING A JOURNAL

A journal can be an enormous aid in our understanding of the unfolding of our daily life and in participating actively in it. It allows us to see patterns in our life and their development over time, as well as focus on our inner experience on a daily basis. It is a workbook and record of our self-discovery; just as a scientist keeps notes on his experiments, we can keep notes on our inner explorations.

Journals are intensely personal; for that reason, I prefer to spend a little money on myself for a hardbound, unlined record book. A good friend, perhaps less materialistic than I, prefers simple spiral notebooks. What does seem important is to have a separate and specific book in which to keep one's journal so that it does not get lost or scattered. The written exercises and drawings in this book will help get you started.

Formatting Your Journal

The format of the journal is also personal. The Intensive Journal as taught by Ira Progoff and his associates has an organized structure with different sections for different purposes, such as relationships, dreams, and theoretical work.[1] Some people find it helpful to create such a format for their journals.

Other journal keepers simply enter thoughts and feelings as they come, keeping track only by date of entry. They see the purpose as the process of recording thoughts and feelings as they occur. Reading at a later time what we have written is of value, too, but concern about formatting to make that easier may interfere with the flow of thoughts and feelings. Somehow writing it down "just as it comes" breaks into cycles of worry and distress, moves us into the Observer, and opens up new perspectives.

Journals are a good place to record drawings like the ones in the previous and following exercises. "Writing it down" may occur in a form other than words. This is one reason I recommend unlined paper. On an unlined page, you may also feel more freedom to write as large or as small or as *scribbled* as you need to express your feelings.

∞

Free Drawing

In your journal or on a large piece of paper, draw freely and without a plan. Use crayons, oil pastels, marking pens, or colored chalk. Pick up whatever color attracts your attention first and watch what your hand does with it. Then take another color and watch again. As a picture begins to form, you may get more specific ideas and want to work for a particular effect. Allow this, but be loose about it. Your unconscious may want to lead you in an unexpected direction, and it is best if you are ready to go along.

Let go of your concern that your drawing be "artistic" or well rendered. Your purpose here is simply to see what comes. If the spirit moves you, do more than one drawing.

When you are finished, study your drawing and see what you see. Write in your journal about any feelings the drawing evokes, or draw again to express them. Look at your drawing as a symbolic statement of your present reality. See if it contains any messages or guidance for you.

∞

Draw Every Day

For a while, try doing a drawing every day at the same time. This will help you loosen up this faculty and give you a progression of images from which to learn about yourself. You can also do drawings in response to specific inner questions, as in most of the drawing exercises in this book. But don't always limit yourself to specific questions; your unconscious may have something more to tell you.

If you feel comfortable doing so, share your drawings with a trusted friend or with your therapist. The other person may see things you have missed and have questions that can deepen your understanding of the wisdom contained in your drawings.

DREAMING

People have looked to their dreams for guidance from earliest times, believing they contained wisdom from the spirit world beyond our normal consciousness. Now we believe they contain information from our own unconscious. Because our reality is so much affected by our inner experience, dreams are extremely important to our understanding of our present situation as well as to our ongoing process of growth. They give us clues about what is going on around us, too, because we pick up much more information from our environment than we can possibly be conscious of during the day. Dreams can teach us how much we are affected by the world around us and give us guidance on personally appropriate actions we might take.

The Power of Dreams

Black Elk taught about the power of dreams; in his tradition, dreams were treated as messages from the Great Spirit.[2]

Particularly powerful dreams, especially those of a shaman, were often enacted ceremonially by the community in order that their teachings might be fully understood and integrated.

We can facilitate the transformative power of our dreams on a personal level by bringing them more into consciousness in our waking life and acknowledging their significance. Retelling dreams and recording them in a dream journal helps to make them more a part of our waking reality.

We can go further, however, through various kinds of "dream work." These techniques are especially useful when dealing with unpleasant or recurring dreams whose messages are difficult to discover.

In one Gestalt therapy approach, you identify with various figures in the dream and speak (or write) from their perspectives. ("I am a fire burning up my house. I am hot and roaring and angry.") This technique is based on the assumption that all figures and objects in a dream reflect parts of the dreamer's psyche. It differs from a cognitive analysis in that you "try on" the various parts of yourself that are reflected in the dream and experience their interaction within yourself. Insight and transformation may occur spontaneously when this is done.

Carl Jung explored the phenomenon of the repressed male or female in each of us. He called the repressed feminine in men "the anima" and the repressed male in women "the animus." Combining this notion with the Gestalt technique suggested above would have us identify and speak from the point of view of any opposite-sex figure in our dreams, especially figures of spouses, lovers, or close partners. We may discover qualities or energies within us that are yearning for release, recognition, and expression.

Transforming a Nightmare

Dreams can also be used as the beginning of imagery work. Simply relax, focus within, and allow your dream to continue in imagery, replaying the dream as it occurred and going on from where it ended. Or you can try out an alternative turn of events. You may dialogue with various figures and try out various ways of getting to know and befriend fearful or antagonistic figures. In this way, a nightmare can be transformed into a reunion with repressed and valuable energies.

Years ago when my children were small, I dreamed I was on a beach with my husband and children. My husband was accosted and beaten by two thugs who dragged him out into the surf to drown him. I wanted to go to his rescue but was afraid to leave my children unattended. I awoke torn by conflicting fears. Immediately, I consciously went back into the dream. This time I imagined my husband using the martial art aikido (which he was studying at the time) to ward off his attackers with ease. I was able to put my fears, and my body, to rest quite soon with this approach. The next day, I replayed both versions of the dream, first identifying with my husband (my animus?) and then with the thugs (who may have reflected fears I had of my male energies). Although I did not do so at the time, it might have been useful as well to take the parts of the two children; they probably represented my own inner child. The work I did, however, left me empowered and energized instead of terrified by the dream.

Dream work is a large field and I will not attempt to do more than outline a couple of approaches as I have here. The bibliography contains a partial list of books that can guide you in integrating your dreams into your expanding understanding of your inner and outer reality.

YOUR AUTOBIOGRAPHY

Our past is part of our present. Every thought and feeling we have now has associations in the past. Our emotional response to daily events has as much to do with past experiences, both pleasant and unpleasant, as it has to do with what is actually happening in the moment. If we want to fully comprehend the present, we need to remember and understand the past.

Writing an autobiography is one way to re-own your past. If you undertake such a project, a few guidelines may help: write an emotional biography rather than a factual one. Write about how you remember seeing and feeling, rather than about information others may have told you. As you write, you may remember more and more. Trust your memories, even if they don't make sense. What you are describing is your inner reality, which no one has the right to contradict. For example, if you felt abused as a child, you were abused, even if your parents considered their actions to be justified "discipline."

A written autobiography can be very helpful in working with a therapist, giving you both a place to begin and a resource for your ongoing explorations. If you have no therapist, you can be your own, to some extent. Reread your autobiography from the compassionate viewpoint of the Observer (see chapter 1, pages 15-17). You may begin to see patterns from your past that you unconsciously allow to affect your choices now. You may see the interrelationships between your own life and larger political, economic, and natural forces around you. You may begin to heal some of the wounds of the past and free yourself in the present for more creative, constructive action. You may appreciate more deeply your strengths and your resilience in the face of trauma and defeat. Further approaches to healing wounds of the past are shared in chapters 7 and 8.

ACCEPTING WHERE WE ARE NOW

Perhaps the greatest challenge in this process of becoming aware of our present existential reality is to accept ourselves exactly as we are, without judgement, blame, or denial. We also need a sense of acceptance of the present situation, with all its pain and beauty, no matter how little or much we like it.

Acceptance does not mean resignation or even approval; we do not have to give up hope for change. Acceptance is simply a realistic recognition of things being the way they are and a willingness to work from that base. Acceptance is always the first step in healing, as paradoxical as that may seem. We need to work with ourselves and with others from where we actually are now, not from where we would like to be.

Piero Ferrucci, in his beautiful book *What We May Be,* writes that acceptance is "the quickest and most practical way to free oneself from a difficult situation, while rebellion inexorably tightens the knot."[3] This is because rebellion is a reaction to the situation, involving little or no understanding of the dynamics of the situation or possible alternative responses. It tends to feed energy into the undesirable situation, creating a vicious circle of action and reaction. When we move toward acceptance, however, we shift "from a reactive to a cognitive attitude." This means "we start seeing life as a training school" in which our current situation can "teach us exactly what we need to learn." Ferrucci offers the following exercise for practicing acceptance.[4]

∞

Acceptance

1.

Think of something in your life for which you feel, or have felt, grateful. It can be the presence of a person you love, a talent you have, a sense of physical well-being, the beauty of a flower, or the like. Imagine it vividly, appreciate it, think of what it gives you and what you can learn from it. . . .

2.

Now think of something (or somebody) you would like to avoid in your life. Again, imagine it, and watch closely any reactions you have. Watch them as they emerge, without trying to stop them. Observe your habitual strategy of nonacceptance and how it works at the level of your body, your feelings, and your mind. . . .

3.

Now suppose that life is guiding you by communicating with you in a code language made up of situations and events. What is the message contained in the situation or event you have chosen? . . .

4.

Now return to whatever it was you felt grateful for. Imagine it once more, think of it with appreciation, and be as fully aware as you can of your acceptance. . . .

5.

Now switch back again to the unpleasant situation, bringing with you the accepting attitude you have aroused. Acknowledge the temporary inevitability of this unpleasant situation. Realize that the same universe that produced what was pleasant also produced the unpleasant, and assume—if you feel ready and are willing—an attitude of conscious, deliberate acceptance.

∞

LIFE AS IT IS

Zen teacher Charlotte Joko Beck says, "There is one thing in life that you can always rely on: life being as it is. . . . Life is always going to be the way it is. . . . Trust in things being as they are is the secret of life."[5] This is a kind of radical acceptance that most of us would think impossible. Yet perhaps we can at least move in that direction. I am reminded of another Zen teaching: "The Great Way is not difficult, for those who have no preferences." While we may still have our preferences, we can find greater ease in living through acceptance—of our own personal imperfections, and of the many troubling situations in our world.

3. Strengthening Our Center

*A*S WE GROW IN AWARENESS, we face feelings, ideas, and behaviors that are troubling to us. Even with our increasing ability to accept ourselves, these feelings and perceptions can be very upsetting. We have not gone unconscious without reason; there is much pain, shame, and despair we would rather not include in our "reality." Our growing awareness may also encompass feelings of joy, surges of energy, and exciting new ideas that can be unnerving and distracting to our daily lives. We may even start to close down our awareness to regain some sense of control.

If we can remain calmly at center, we will be better prepared to accept, assimilate, and grow with all these experiences. Models and principles of centering can help us understand the process, while techniques and exercises train our "psychological muscles" to return to center with increasing ease.

THE HUB OF OUR POWER

What do we mean by "center" and "centering"? These words are being used more and more commonly to describe an experience many people have of being "at the center" of their lives. Our center is a point of balance and integration; it is the hub of our power and awareness.

Imagine yourself as a wagon wheel, with the spokes representing the various qualities and faculties of your psyche. If you are operating from the edge of your wheel, you have only the spokes of the wheel that end in that area readily available for use. If you operate from the center, however, all your spokes are equally available to you.

I have had the experience many times of losing my center, usually in a social interaction in which I am trying unconsciously to conform to vague group norms or to please and attract someone. Or I may be engrossed in planning some project, usually with an element of worry. In either case, something helps me become aware of what is happening; maybe I stumble, or embarrass myself with an inappropriate remark. At the moment I become aware, I sense that my energy is focused approximately a foot and a half out in front of me. I feel off-balance, awkward, and out of control. I need to take a deep breath and bring my energy and focus back inside myself, to center.

Being centered does not mean being "self-centered" in the usual sense of the term. When my energy is centered within me, I am aware of what is going on outside, and I can respond in a balanced and intelligent way. When I am centered, I am self-contained, not self-absorbed. In fact, I am far more able to respond "unselfishly" to others.

IDENTIFICATION AND DISIDENTIFICATION

To operate from the hub of the wheel means changing our sense of who we are, our basic "identification." Do we think of ourselves as only this or that quality, this or that spoke? Or do we think of ourselves as the hub, or even as the whole wheel?

How we identify ourselves may either limit us or challenge

us to expand our capacities. When we identify with one or another part of ourselves, with a point of view, an emotion, or bodily sensation, we are limited in our self-image, our world-view, our whole sense of reality. We are limited in how well we can respond to the inevitable shifts and changes of our lives. We believe we can only think, feel, and act in one way, sometimes even saying to ourselves and others, "This is just the way I am!"

Choosing Our Perspective and Behavior

When we are able to "dis-identify" from these parts of ourselves, we free ourselves to choose our perspective and behavior from a broader range of possibilities, realizing that we don't have to be, or act, just one way. "Disidentification" means moving our sense of identity out of a box into the open air. When we disidentify from a limited part of ourselves, our sense of who we are can expand. We can begin to "identify" with the whole of our extraordinary potential. We can begin to express our deepest values and essential qualities in our actions instead of getting caught up in the melodrama.

If I am feeling angry, for example, I may *identify* with that anger; I may think of myself as "an angry person" and not as a loving one. I imagine I have no choice but to be angry. If I can *disidentify* from my feeling of anger, I realize that although anger is definitely an important part of my experience in the moment, I am also feeling and thinking a lot of other things. I am also loving, fearful, thoughtful, empathetic, strong, confused, and much more. And I can make choices based on all these experiences of myself in the moment.

Disidentification can be easily confused with the experience of separating ourselves from our experience—disowning our feelings, thoughts, and bodily sensations. Most of us suppress feelings, thoughts, and bodily sensations at times, often to the point where we don't even know of their existence. Disowning and suppressing our feelings, thoughts, and sensations cut us off from our inner resources instead of opening us up to the whole of our being.

When we truly disidentify from an experience, we are usually even more vividly aware of it. We own the various parts of ourselves more fully because we no longer feel trapped in them. We experience our identity being enlarged rather than restricted. We embrace all our thoughts, feelings, and sensations while sensing that our identity is not limited to those passing experiences.

In the following exercise, you can explore for yourself the subtleties of disidentification and perhaps discover a more inclusive and enduring sense of identity, of "I-ness."

∞

Identification Exercise

Sit in a comfortable position, relax your body, and allow your breathing to become slow and deep. Read each paragraph slowly, then close your eyes and pay attention to your inner responses.

Take a few minutes to observe your body. What is your body? How do you experience it? Notice any sensations you have in your body: pain, tension, ease, motion, irritation, expansion and contraction, warmth, pleasure. Notice how these sensations change from moment to moment.

Now notice how you can change your sensations. Tense your muscles in one area, notice how it feels, and then relax the muscles. Experiment with other ways of affecting your sensations.

Consider these questions for a few moments: *Are these sensations who I am? When my body sensations change, do "I" change too? If so, how? Who is the "I" who can affect my body sensations, at least to some extent? Who am I in relation to my body sensations? . . .*

Now move your attention to your emotions, your feelings. Notice them, name the ones you can: fear, confusion, attraction, joy, sorrow, frustration, etc. Keep the strongest feeling in the center of your attention for a while, and see what happens. Notice if it changes. Notice if other feelings arise. . . .

Now notice how you can change your emotions. Think about something very exciting and see how your feelings respond. Experiment with other ways of affecting your emotions. . . .

Consider these questions for a few minutes: *Are these feelings who I am? When my feelings change, do "I" change too? If so, how? Who is the "I" who can choose my feelings, at least to some extent? Who am I in relation to my feelings? . . .*

To do this exercise, you have been using what we call "the mind." Take a few minutes now to watch your "mind." How do you do this? Notice your thoughts as they come and go. Notice the forms they take: images, words, impressions, questions, conclusions, memories, problems, perceptions, etc. Notice any difficulties you have "observing" your thoughts.

Now experiment with changing and directing your thoughts. Pick a word and think about its meaning for a few moments. Now think about what you did right after you got up this morning. Try other means to change your thoughts.

Consider these questions for a few minutes: *Are these thoughts who I am? When my thoughts change, do "I" change too? How? Who is the "I" who seems to be able to direct my thoughts, at least to some extent? Who am I in relation to my thoughts, my "mind"? . . .*

Now pay attention to all of these: sensations, feelings, and thoughts. How do you experience your sense of self in relation to these ongoing, changing experiences? Take some time to sit with this question, allowing any new understandings and perspectives to emerge from within.

∞

WHO AM I?

We must each come to our own unique understanding of who we are, gleaned from our own experience and ideas shared by others. I have come to think of myself, most essentially, as a center of consciousness and will, distinct but not separate from my sensations, feelings, and thoughts. I am "I," capable of observing and changing how I think and feel and act. I am one who is aware, one who chooses, within the vast interconnecting web of being.

WHAT IS SELF?

Assagioli describes the self in the following way. Notice that here he uses a lower case *s*; he is referring to what we will call the "I" or the "personal self."

At the heart of the self there is both an active and a passive element, an agent and a spectator. Self-consciousness involves our being a witness—a pure, objective, loving witness—to what is happening within and without. In this sense, the self is not a dynamic in itself but a point of witness, a spectator, an observer who watches the flow. But there is another part of the inner self—the will-er or directing agent—that actively intervenes to orchestrate the various functions and energies of the personality, to make commitments and to instigate action in the external world. So, at the center of the self, there is a unity of . . . will and love, action and observation.[1]

Let's distinguish "self" from "ego" as it is commonly conceived. Ego may imply pride, selfishness, concern with personal glory, and aggrandizement. The self we are trying to describe is without qualities. It is pure awareness, without content; the source of the energy of intention, choice, or will.

The Spiritual Source Within Us

As we identify ourselves more closely with the personal self, the "I," we may feel or sense an even deeper identity, a spiritual Source within us and encompassing us. This "beingness" has been given various names through the ages: Spirit, Soul, Self, Atman, Tao, No-self. In psychosynthesis and in other transpersonal psychologies, this underlying mysterious Presence is called Self, or Higher Self. Self transcends our personality, our situation in life, our roles, our gender. Yet Self is present no matter how confused, in pain, lost, or broken we may feel. Its energy is available for guidance and support as we make our way through our lives, in these bodies, with these personalities, within whatever situations we find ourselves. I believe "Self" is akin to the "Higher Power" that is the source of healing for recovering alcoholics and others in Twelve Step programs of recovery.

The personal self or "I" is a reflection or expression of Self at the level of the personality. Self, in turn, may be thought to be an expression of a larger Whole, called among other names Universal Being. Self is the interface between the individual and the Whole. It is through experiences of Self that we are in union with our fellow humans and with the whole of creation. We might even name it "Ecological Self."

Joanna Macy speaks to this larger sense of self in *World as Lover, World as Self*:

> The way we define and delimit the self is arbitrary. We can place it between our ears and have it looking out from our eyes, or we can widen it to include the air we breathe, or, at other moments, we can cast its boundaries farther to include the oxygen-giving trees and plankton, our external lungs, and beyond them the web of life in which they are sustained.[2]

At rare and precious moments in life we may experience this sense of oneness and unity with all of life. These moments inspire us to realign our priorities and values and clear away the underbrush in our personalities so that we may live more fully from a perspective of wholeness and interconnectedness.

∞

Letter to Self

On a piece of stationery or in your journal, write a letter to your Self. Begin with the date and a greeting as you would any letter: "Dear Self" (or whatever name you prefer). Then simply write as honestly and openly as you can. Imagine that you are writing to your most trusted and understanding friend. You can discuss anything you wish in your letter: your questions, thoughts, and feelings about your Self; problems, crises, or decisions you are facing in your life; plans and creative projects; other aspects of your life.

You may find your feelings and perspectives change in the course of the letter. Let your writing reflect that. When you feel finished, sign your name with whatever closing you wish to use.[3]

∞

The formality of a letter helps focus your attention on your "relationship" with Self. It creates a channel for energy to flow to your personality and helps identify any feelings or ideas that may be blocking that flow. Moreover, you may find yourself receiving "answers" to your letters in dreams, sudden insights, remarks from friends, and reading. Writing a letter every day for a period of time is a powerful discipline in centering.

MEDITATION

The power of meditation has become common knowledge among people involved in personal and spiritual growth. I use the word here in its broadest sense, referring to the whole spectrum of practices of silent, inner focus that enhance self-awareness, relaxation, and centeredness. One form or another of meditation may already be a part of your life.

Some who seek personal and spiritual growth find meditation difficult, however. They may have a narrow understanding of what it is and may be intimidated by the apparent rigors that its practitioners seem to endure. No matter what its form, meditation is a discipline, requiring training and experience. But there are gentler approaches, and some are easier than others for Westerners. One may begin with an "easy" approach and move on to a more rigorous method later.

Many Approaches to Meditation

I will not try to describe all the possible approaches to meditation; that would be a book unto itself. There are several such books already available; I recommend Ram Dass's *Journey of Awakening*.[4] Others are listed in the bibliography. Many teachers and centers are available throughout the world.

A form of meditation recommended by the founder of psychosynthesis, Roberto Assagioli, is called "creative meditation." It is a kind of focused thinking centered on a seed thought or quality, and is based on some practices of Raja Yoga in the Hindu tradition. It is described in detail in chapter 10.

For strengthening our center, the simplest practice of meditation is probably the best—just taking time to sit with no other agenda than being here now. Watching the breath. Watching the feelings arise and change. Watching the judgements, questions, interpretations, and images as they pass through the mind. Returning always to the breath.

In meditation we learn to observe and direct our minds and feelings through choice instead of allowing them to wander and react the way we do most of the time. Meditation helps us to practice nonjudgemental self-observation and acceptance. Thus we experience compassion and firmness toward our feelings, desires, thoughts, and the various parts of our personalities. In other words, we develop our will, our inherent capacity for self-determination in our thoughts, feelings, and actions.

PRESENCE

When we are centered, we are present to our whole selves and to the world around us. We are not hiding feelings, judgements, and knowledge from ourselves or others. We are available to respond with love, wisdom, and clarity to whatever occurs inside or out. Presence alone can be healing; how freeing to know that we don't have to do anything except just be here with our emotions, thoughts, imagination, intuition; just be here in our bodies, listening, seeing, feeling, caring! Healing and constructive action arise spontaneously when we are truly present.

Paradoxically, presence rests on nonattachment, the letting go of preconceptions about what ought to occur and the desire for some kind of measurable success. The challenge is to be involved in life without getting entangled, to keep our understanding and perceptions broad rather than narrowed down to one small aspect or point of view.

Releasing Things to Their Destinies

Involvement and nonattachment may seem to contradict one another. How can we really be with someone or be involved in some activity, yet not care what happens (or at least not let our caring get in the way)? To be both involved and detached demands that we hold a broad view, one that enables us to trust in life and its unfolding. From our limited human perspective we do not really know if one outcome is better than another, although we usually have our preferences. Releasing situations, problems, and people to their unfolding destinies keeps us from complicating things with our limited ideas of what should happen. Working for a particular outcome may help structure our activities, but if we become too attached to that outcome, we may prevent something even better from happening, something we cannot foresee.

A Mother's Concern

Anyone who is a parent knows how difficult it is to keep this balance between involvement and detachment. We fervently want what is best for our children, and we usually assume that what we think is best actually is. I recall a time when my husband and I were living with our two sons, an infant and a three-year-old, in a somewhat decrepit old adobe house in northern New Mexico. We had very little money because my husband was struggling to start a private practice as a psychotherapist, and we had moved into the house as caretakers in order to make ends meet.

One day when I was visiting my mother, who lived in a nearby town, she began to cry, saying that she was so worried about me and knew I must be miserable. I was amazed, because I was as happy as I had ever been in my life. I was mothering two beautiful children, I lived in the country in a beautiful old house filled with good spirits, and my husband and I were very close to each other. I felt very connected to the basic rhythms of life, and the attendant hardships were quite tolerable. My mother, however, was basing her sense of what was best for me on the external situation alone. It was hard for her to trust that the hardships I faced were completely within my capacities to handle—indeed, that they were part of my learning and growing at that time. She wanted to rescue me from my own destiny.

A Father's Compassionate Detachment

My husband, Jim, recalls a time when our older son, Greg, was injured in a bicycle accident and had a deep cut on his cheek. Jim helped immobilize Greg while the doctor anesthetized the area and took stitches. Jim was certainly involved in the process, but he had to be compassionately detached from Greg's fear and pain in order to assist the doctor. His compassionate detachment was also reassuring and calming to Greg.

To be present to our children, or anyone else, means to respect and honor their process of growth and learning, no matter how painful it may be at times. We support them, we let them know that we feel their pain too, but we don't try to rescue them from the way life is. As in my case, they may be much better off than we realize anyway! And if they are in trouble, they are more likely to turn to us for help if they know we will not try to impose our own sense of "what is best" on them, but rather help them discover that for themselves.

The following exercise may help you experience the power of being present, alone and with others. Walter Polt and I developed it when we worked together at Intermountain Associates in New Mexico.

∞

The Perfect Companion

Take a few minutes now to find a comfortable, alert position and to relax. Close your eyes and pay attention to your inner experience. . . .

Remember a time in the recent past when you were in an emotional crisis or facing a difficult decision. Relive that experience as fully as you can now. Recall how your body felt, what kinds of postures or movements you might have used. . . . What were your feelings? . . . What were your thoughts and how did your mind work? . . . How did the world in general look to you from within this experience? . . .

Now imagine a companion you would have liked to have with you, someone whom you could trust and with whom you would feel completely comfortable, even in this trying time. This companion may or may not remind you of friends you already know, yet there is something familiar about her or him. Take some time to develop a sense of this companion. . . .

What are the qualities of this person with whom you would choose to share your turmoil and distress? . . . How would he or she respond to you? What, if anything, might be said? What would she or he communicate without words? . . .

Take time to explore this person's presence, making any changes in the image that you need in order to be completely comfortable. . . .

If you are willing to take another step, imagine that *you are* this perfect companion, that those qualities are yours. Try looking back at yourself in crisis and experience what feelings and thoughts you have from this perspective about

yourself in crisis. . . . What might you say to yourself about
how you see yourself in crisis from this perspective or about
your willingness and attitude in being there? . . .

Imagine bringing the qualities and attitudes of your imagined companion into your relationships with others, your
family and friends, people at work and in the community.
Imagine being with yourself in this way. . . . How would it be
to bring these qualities and attitudes into play when you
think about people and events in other parts of the world? . . .

Take time to allow this experience its full impact, and
then make some notes in your journal.

We can become more balanced and centered simply by disidentifying from the changing experiences of sensations, feelings, and thoughts. Building our sense of relationship with
Self through writing and meditation and developing presence
with ourselves and with others through imagery and practice
will also help us in achieving a sense of being balanced and
centered. In these ways, we strengthen the center or hub of
our wheel and become more able to cope with the demands of
daily life, the challenges of our ongoing development as whole
human beings, and the profound problems facing the human
race.

4. What's Possible?

STRENGTHENING OUR CENTER is a starting place for exploring our vast potential as human beings. When we are centered, we are in a better position to see both our strengths and our limitations, to accept the reality of our dreams and visions, and to see what needs to be done to fulfill them.

To paraphrase the Bard, Are we the stuff that dreams are made of? The answer is "Yes! Most certainly, yes!" In fact, each of us has potential talents, abilities, wisdom, and power that we may not have yet imagined. In this chapter, we consider a model of the human psyche that specifically includes our potentials, inspirations, and dreams.

We are so much more than who we have thought we are and what we have done up to now. Individually and collectively, we have the capacity to learn new ways of thinking that will help us to better understand ourselves and the world. We can devise new approaches to our personal and collective problems. We can acquire new skills for mastery and creativity in our world. We can more fully love and enjoy living. We can build more nurturing relationships and move toward greater harmony—personally, socially, and spiritually—with our planet.

Perhaps you have already learned a new way of thinking or a new approach from the work we have done so far. It might be helpful to look over your experience in reading the previous chapters and recall your insights, your moments of "aha!" Notice how these insights have affected the way you think about yourself or the way you approach certain problems. You have already uncovered capacities within yourself that you may not have known were there.

In mid-twentieth century, a new view of human nature gave rise to what is called "humanistic" and "transpersonal" psychology. Both movements support the notion that we can do much better than merely "adjusting" ourselves to what is generally considered to be normal, to some sort of socially acceptable standard of "adequate" mental health. Humanistic and transpersonal psychologists believe that psychology has a responsibility to help move people beyond normalcy. By studying super-healthy people, called "self-actualizers" by transpersonal psychologist Abraham Maslow, these psychologists seek to discover what makes people capable of extraordinary achievement in art, science, athletics, and leadership.

We Can Become Self-Actualizers

What they have been finding is that most of us are capable of thinking and doing far more than we have. We are limited mainly by our beliefs about ourselves, beliefs often acquired in childhood and through social pressure as adults. As we change these beliefs and build our self-esteem, we too can become self-actualizers and do what we previously would have considered to be extraordinary and out of our reach.

In response to the needs of our endangered planet, we have undertaken a journey toward Self-realization. The next step is to assess our inborn talents and gifts. To do that, we must first accept the possibility that such potentials exist, beyond what we now know about ourselves. If we don't think something is possible, we are not likely to spend any time trying it out. Let's begin with a guided journey of our unconscious inner world where our hidden capacities may lie.

⚭

Levels of Consciousness

1.

Take a moment to focus your attention inside, to where you are right now. Notice what you are aware of physically, both within your body and in your immediate environment: what do you experience through your senses? . . .

Notice what feelings are present, and what issues or concerns are on your mind. . . .

When your mind wanders a bit, where does it go? . . .

See how much you can be aware of all at once; let your attention expand as much as possible. . . .

Then, for a short while, focus your attention on a single sensation, feeling, or thought, shutting out everything else as best you can. . . .

If you were to contain all of this within an imaginary circle, that circle would be your immediate field of awareness. Its contents shift and change, moment to moment. The size of the field can even expand and contract. Take a few moments to experiment with expanding and contracting your attention. . . .

Both conditions are of value in different situations. Notice your ability to expand and contract your field of awareness at will.

2.

Now recall what you had for breakfast this morning (even if it was nothing). . . . Where was that information just before you recalled it? Where do you keep phone numbers, people's names, recent events, skills that are not being used in the moment? Take a few moments to sense "where" these memories reside when you are not using them. . . .

This aspect of the unconscious is called the *middle unconscious*. Its contents are readily available to our conscious mind, passing in and out of awareness as if through a permeable membrane. Watch this process for a few moments, noticing thoughts, associations, and memories that come into your awareness and then are replaced by others. . . .

3.

Next, see if you can become aware of a mysterious region of your inner experience that is largely unknown to you. From time to time, impulses, desires, strong feelings such as depression or anger arise from this region, often without your knowing why. . . .

This is the *basic unconscious,* the repository of your basic drives and processes, and of painful or confusing feelings you have repressed in order to survive. Here reside the monsters of your nightmares, your irrational fears, resentments, and anger. And in this region reside the primal energies that connect you to the animal kingdom and to life itself.

For a few moments, allow yourself to acknowledge this dimension of your unconscious. . . .

Perhaps you can move your field of awareness closer to this domain and allow some hints of its contents to come to your attention. . . .

Acknowledge its guardianship of your basic life processes and its value in keeping memories and feelings out of your immediate awareness until you are ready to confront and integrate them. . . .

Now return your attention to what feels like your center, following your breath and moment-to-moment feelings and sensations for a short while. . . .

4.

When you feel ready, move your awareness toward yet another region of your unconscious, toward the experience of inspiration, imagination, or insight. Where are your ideas before they come to you? Where do your dreams come from? . . .

Where lie the solutions to your present dilemmas, solutions that you sense you will find in due time? . . . Where are your aspirations, your compassion, your wisdom, when you have temporarily lost touch with them or not yet tapped their power? . . .

Imagine moving your field of awareness closer to this domain, so that you can have a stronger sense of the energies and patterns within it.

This is your *superconscious,* or *higher unconscious.* Its energies and archetypal patterns are just as real and powerful as those from the basic unconscious. Affirm for a few moments the existence of this realm within your unconscious, available to you for guidance whenever needed. Allow whatever images come to mind to portray this dimension to you. . . .

Then, once again, return your awareness to the sense of center, of self. Take a few more moments to simply breathe, notice your sensations, feelings, thoughts. . . .

∽

THE "EGG"

The four aspects of consciousness we have just explored are depicted in the oval diagram, nicknamed the "egg," a psychosynthesis model of our conscious and unconscious mind. (See figure 1.) These four aspects are shown as regions separated by dotted lines to indicate that no true boundaries exist between them. Feelings, thoughts, images, energies, and other contents of consciousness can move in and out of each region freely. (In fact, there are no "regions"; all these contents are mixed up together. But to give us a sense of the different kinds, the oval diagram divides them into categories.)

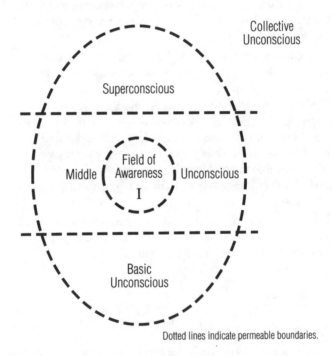

Dotted lines indicate permeable boundaries.

Figure 1 – Oval Diagram

The Middle Unconscious

The "field of awareness" is the circle in the center, with "I" (personal self) at its center. This circle represents whatever we are thinking, feeling, and sensing at the present moment. The field of awareness is surrounded by the "middle unconscious," a neutral area of recently forgotten and easily recalled experience that Freud called the "preconscious." The middle unconscious is a kind of "holding" area for our field of awareness, so we don't have to focus on too many thoughts, feelings, impressions, and associations at one time.

The Basic Unconscious

At the bottom of the oval is the basic unconscious, containing the basic physical and psychological patterns that direct the life of the body. This is the control center for our heartbeat, breathing, digestion, and all the other automatic processes that keep us alive. This region holds our fundamental drives, such as sexuality and other survival instincts.

The basic unconscious also contains repressed desires, emotions, and traumas. This is the region of the unconscious that Freud described so well, which he called simply the unconscious. When we do deep therapeutic work, we are usually exploring patterns and memories from the basic unconscious.

The Superconscious

In a sense, the basic unconscious contains our past, and the superconscious, in the upper region of the oval, our future. The superconscious carries our creativity and intuition, and our promptings to love, compassion, and service; it carries our highest values and inspirations, spiritual energies, and the "blueprints" for our future growth. It is the repository of our potential, our aspirations and dreams.

Growing Whole

For years, this aspect of the unconscious was largely ignored. Many psychologists considered the manifestations of superconscious, such as creativity or the desire to help others, to be simply "sublimated" sexuality and/or aggression. Now many humanistic and transpersonal psychologists recognize that we humans "naturally" have drives toward love, creativity, and wisdom that exist in their own right. Repression of these drives can have just as damaging an effect on mental health as repression of sexuality or other basic drives. The oval diagram represents the importance of this aspect of the unconscious by assigning it an area of its own.

The Collective Unconscious

Around the outside of the oval is the region of the collective unconscious, the patterns of unconscious feeling and thought that we share with those around us. We can see effects of the collective unconscious in quite tangible ways: advertising that appeals to basic desires that many people have in common, symbols that bring out a similar response from everyone in a culture. There may even be a collective unconscious shared by all human beings. This is the theory of Carl Jung's "archetype," a universal pattern of response to the elements of life shared by all people, such as mother, father, water, fire, earth, and sky.

The collective unconscious has all the levels of the individual unconscious: basic, middle, and superconscious. We share common demons and common aspirations, some of which seem to appear in all cultures. Those of us working in areas of social change draw on images from the collective superconscious to inspire others, using pictures of people holding hands, smiles, mothers and babies, and photographs of the Earth from space. The makers of horror movies make use (for good or for ill) of the collective basic unconscious, exploiting symbols such as sharks, ghosts, and "things that go bump in the night."

It is vital to our development as whole human beings that we become aware of material from all levels of the unconscious, that we accept all these energies as good and healthy aspects of ourselves, and that we use them wisely. Rather than merely being victims of desires, conditioned responses, and unconscious drives, we each have the ability to be the orchestrator of our lives, observing and acting from the center of our lives.

Let's keep in mind that models such as this are only rough approximations of reality. They are useful only to the extent that they speak to your experience and suggest new possibilities. The purpose of the egg diagram is to reveal to us the possibility of enormous potentials—in the superconscious, in the basic unconscious, and in the collective unconscious—organized and energized by Self.[1]

You might experiment with adapting this model or creating your own model for your experience of the dimensions of the unconscious and Self.

THE REPRESSION OF THE SUBLIME

Accepting our potentials is not so easy. We resist being who we really are for a number of reasons. It seems like an awesome responsibility to be as great as we may be; who needs more expectations and judgements piled up on them? It seems difficult enough to measure up to the normal range of family and social expectations, and we may already feel our freedom to live and play is severely limited. Why add more to these demands?

And what if we fail? What if our belief about our capacities is unrealistic and we attempt more than we can achieve? We might make fools of ourselves, or worse yet, really damage our reputation within the community. We might even lose our jobs, our financial security, our chances for advancement within our community or workplace.

The Courage to Talk About Values

To aspire to wisdom, altruism, hope, peace, generosity, and compassion in today's world may seem foolish and weak to some. Because much of our society is built on the assumption that one group or individual must dominate others to survive and progress, values such as these are often ridiculed and repressed. They may be talked about on Saturday or Sunday morning within the confines of one's place of worship, but by and large, they are discounted the rest of the week. It takes considerable courage to talk about such values in the face of this social pressure, as well as considerable skill and determination to build one's life around them.

Consider for a moment, however, what would happen if you were to suddenly manifest a new artistic talent in your life, or if you became aware of a strong pull to serve humankind in a self-sacrificing way. How would this disrupt your life? How would your family members and friends react to this change? What kind of advice would you be likely to receive from a financial advisor or business partner?

A few years ago, my husband had two conversations about my work as the organizer of what was then called the Soviet Psychosynthesis Project. This project involved many hours of unpaid work on my part, as well as weeks of travel to the former Soviet Union. My father-in-law said to my husband, "Well, if it's not lucrative, I don't know why she does it." Our insurance agent said, "I'm sure it's wonderful work, but when she gets sick, those people aren't going to come over here and take care of her." Both of these men were expressing widely held beliefs about the practicality of pursuing dreams, especially those involving unpaid service. Those beliefs encourage us to repress our dreams and impulses to serve in favor of making money and living "sensibly."

On the other hand, we may think that others around us share our values but that we as individuals are just not good enough, smart enough, or ambitious enough to do what we would like to do. Our aspirations may seem to be unreachable goals, and yet we may criticize ourselves for our failure to live up to them.

Repressing Our Dreams Can Be Unhealthy

Any ceiling we place on our aspirations cripples us as severely as the repression of our more primitive desires and energies. Frank Haronian, a psychosynthesis theorist, used the phrase "the repression of the sublime" to describe the tendency to deny our potential. When we do this to ourselves, we begin to wither inside. Most often we become depressed, unconsciously grieving the loss of something we sensed but never really knew we had. Sometimes we become angry, lashing out in various ways at a world that has denied us our birthright to be.

We may suffer from a whole range of physical ailments that reflect metaphorically our diseased potentials. Heart trouble, for example, may reflect our unrealized capacity to love or our unspoken heartbreak when we witness suffering and violence. We may heal faster on a physical level when we pay attention to these psychological and spiritual issues in addition to seeking appropriate medical treatment.

Fortunately, this process is reversible. Our potential, however repressed, does not die. Our capacities and values remain
in the superconscious, waiting for us to accept and release
them. Sometimes we have healing to do in order to reverse
long-held patterns of repression and denial, but we also have
remarkable powers to accomplish this healing. Chapters 6, 7,
8, and 9 offer specific tools for facilitating healing. For now it
may be enough for us simply to recognize the existence of the
superconscious and our tendency to repress it. What are your
own tendencies to "repress the sublime"?

OPENING THE DOOR

How do we open the door to this reservoir of potential?
How do we gain access to it and bring all that good energy
into our lives? Recognizing its existence opens the door a
crack, and superconscious energies will begin to seep through
without our conscious assistance. Perhaps we will begin to
have inspiring dreams. Perhaps we will feel a tug to pick up a
musical instrument or art materials long neglected. Perhaps
we will begin study of a new artistic form. Or perhaps we will
find ourselves daydreaming about a community or international project we would like to undertake, or even about a new
career.

It is possible, however, to consciously open the door more
widely and to actively seek out the capacities and energies
we need in our daily lives. Our superconscious is a vast store
of unconscious wisdom that is available to us for guidance.
The skills of awareness, self-observation (chapter 1), self-
identification, and meditation (chapter 3) that we have been
practicing have already helped us gain access to this guidance. We specifically addressed this store of wisdom in writing

a letter to Self (see page 42). And now let's take an inner journey to visit "the Wise Being" who resides in us all.

The Wise Being

Begin by closing your eyes, relaxing your body, and seeking a quiet place within. Focus your awareness on your breathing for a few moments. . . .

Now imagine that you hold a candle before you in a candleholder. Imagine lighting the candle, watching the flame flicker and then grow strong. Watch the flame for a few moments, seeing how it burns stronger and brighter as you watch. . . .

Notice the tiny blue flame at the heart of the larger yellow flame. Focus your attention there, looking deeper and deeper into the heart of it until that is all you see. . . .

In the heart of the tiny blue flame appears the face of a very wise and loving being. Notice the wisdom and the love that radiate from the face and eyes of this being, wisdom and love that are there just for you at this moment. . . .

You may ask this being for advice about anything happening in your life, any issue or concern you have, or what your next steps might be. Ask any question you have and just be receptive to whatever comes, in whatever form. Notice what you feel, see, hear, and sense from the Wise Being. . . .

The Wise Being may have something to tell you besides what you have asked, a special message for you. If you are willing to receive it, tell the Wise Being that this is so and wait for a response. . . .

Turn now and look at any issue in your life, with the Wise Being beside you. Allow yourself to see the situation as the Wise Being sees it. . . .

Perhaps you want to make a choice about your role in the situation, about how you want to be. . . . Tell the Wise Being about your choice. . . .

Imagine yourself carrying out your choice. See how you behave and feel and how others respond to you. . . .

Imagine yourself calling upon the wisdom and love of the Wise Being to help you sustain your choice. . . .

Now take leave of the Wise Being, knowing you can return at any time to find guidance and strength. When you are ready, open your eyes and take time to make some notes about your experience.[2]

∞

Our Creative Imagination

The Wise Being is a symbol of the wisdom and love that lie within your own superconscious. You could not imagine this Being if these qualities were not within you. Where did the words and images come from, if they did not come from your own unconscious?

Some might protest, "Well, I am just making it up." Yes, indeed, and our capacity to make things up—our creative imagination—is responsible for all the achievements of humankind. You can test the value of the guidance you imagined in this exercise by trying it out. Does it help you feel more positive or think about your situation in a new way? Does it help you come to a decision and take action?

Philosophers, poets, scientists, and artists have all thought and written about the human potential. We know the depths of brutality that are possible for humans and also the brilliance and saintliness. To tap into our own potential, however, we need to bring these notions home to ourselves as individuals. We are, each one of us, the stuff that dreams are made of; we each create dreams; and we can and do bring at least some of our dreams into being for the benefit of the world.

What is possible for you now in your life? Now that we have a sense of the unconscious resources available to us, we are ready to explore this question.

5. Setting Our Sights

DREAMS AND VISIONS seem to be essential to the human spirit, yet they are all too often devalued and ignored. We are told by much of the culture around us to be "realistic" and shun fantasy. When our dreams fail—or we fail them—we decide those voices are right, and we reject dreaming in order to spare ourselves disappointment. Unfortunately, in the process, we shut the door on dreams which could be realized or which could lead us in new, creative directions.

Pop psychology urges us to set goals of a tangible nature so that we can measure their attainment, and there is value in that. Such finite goals may indeed serve as milestones for our progress, but, if set prematurely, they can act as limitations for our dreams. Not all our dreams can be captured in concrete goals, because they have an element of mystery, hints of wisdom not yet made conscious. When we compress our dreams into "behavioral objectives," we may squeeze the life out of them.

Consider for a few minutes the dreams and visions you have had for yourself throughout your life. What have they meant to you? How have they inspired you or, conversely, disappointed you?

A DREAM

Dr. Martin Luther King, Jr., inspired millions with his famous speech, "I Have a Dream." His dream was our dream and lives on today. He communicated his dream with words that helped us imagine a better future, a future of equality, love, and harmony. There were no limited goals or timetables to meet, only a vision of what is possible.

> I say to you today, my friends, that in spite of the difficulties and frustrations of the moment I still have a dream. It is a dream deeply rooted in the American dream. I have a dream that one day this nation will rise up and live out the true meaning of its creed: "We hold these truths to be self-evident; that all men are created equal." I have a dream that one day on the red hills of Georgia, sons of former slaves and the sons of former slaveowners will be able to sit down together at the table of brotherhood. I have a dream that one day even the state of Mississippi, a desert state sweltering with the heat of injustice and oppression, will be transformed into an oasis of freedom and justice. . . . I have a dream today.[1]

At every turn of our lives, we have latent capacities waiting in the wings for us to bring them on stage. We have purposes to challenge and motivate us. We have yearnings and hopes. We have images of how we'd like things, and ourselves, to be. So let's take some time to dream and envision. Let's explore the possibilities, the potentials, the growth and creativity that are ready to emerge in your life right now.

∞

What Is Possible for Me Now in My Life?

Have ready a sheet of paper or a page in your journal, drawing materials (either oil pastels, colored markers, or crayons), and a pencil or pen. Sit in a comfortable, upright position and take a few moments to simply breathe, allowing your body to come to rest. . . .

Now quietly observe your feelings and thoughts. Let them be there and let them also come to rest. . . .

Now find a quiet place inside where you can be open, receptive, and patient, where you can receive responses from within. Allow yourself to abide in that place as you contemplate the following questions. Make brief notes about your responses to each question—thoughts, feelings, images, impressions.

1. *What is emerging now in my life?*
2. *What is my next step?*
3. *What is possible for me now?*

Choose the question that seems to speak to you the most. Close your eyes and ask the question again, taking more time to notice any images, sensations, feelings, and thoughts which arise in response. . . .

Use your drawing materials to represent that response in colors, shapes, symbols, or pictures. . . .

Write about any feelings, meanings, messages from the drawing. . . .[2]

∽

Explore the Meanings

When your drawing is finished, explore its subtler meanings as you would a dream. You can share your drawing with a trusted friend, and, in talking about it, you may understand more of its implications. Compare it with the drawing you did in chapter 2 on "Where am I now in my life?" Notice any common themes. You may want to set the drawing aside and take a fresh look at it in a day or two.

Some people find these drawings very inspirational and enjoy putting them up in their homes so they can be reminded of their dreams. Some even frame their drawings, although they are not necessarily "great art." When I have seen such drawings framed, my attention is drawn to them, and I tend to look at them with new respect and care.

This drawing is the second of a series of four we will be working with through the next few chapters. In chapter 6, we'll also examine what gets in the way of our vision, and in chapter 9, what qualities we need to develop. It is not enough to dream our dreams; we need to work with ourselves and our world to realize them, and we will do just that. But first, let's set our sights even more keenly on possibilities and purpose.

PURPOSE

Assagioli believed the first stage in any willed act to be clarification of purpose. Having a sense of purpose certainly lifts our sights beyond the immediate difficulties and helps motivate us to move forward. We may never define exactly what our life's purpose is, but it certainly helps to have a sense of one. Clarifying purpose also opens up a wider array of choices for us, for there is usually more than one way to accomplish a purpose. We may be less confined to specific plans when we have a clear sense of purpose.

∽

Exercise for Exploring Purpose

This exercise is best done with a partner who asks the question "What is your purpose in that?" at each succeeding response. Your partner can even repeat the key words from your last response in asking again for your purpose. For example, if the first question is, "What is my purpose in working with this book?" you might respond, "To know myself better." Then your second question would be, "What is my purpose in knowing myself better?" and you might answer, "To have more control of my life." Your third question would then be, "What is my purpose in having more control of my life?"—and so on.

If you have no partner to work with, you can simply ask yourself the question, note your response, and ask the question again, repeating the key phrases as a partner would. Listen within as you ask, and allow images and feelings to arise, as well as words and thoughts.

First take a few minutes to get comfortable and relaxed. Close your eyes to allow your thoughts and feelings to become quiet and receptive. . . .

Now ask yourself, "What is my purpose in working with this book?"

Take this inside for contemplation, and write down your response. . . .

Now ask yourself, "And what is the purpose of that (whatever you responded to the first question)?"

"And what is the purpose of that?"

"And what is the purpose of that?"

Continue in this manner until you find a sense of purpose that seems to have the greatest meaning and usefulness to your life. Write a clear, concise statement of your deep sense of purpose. . . .

Take some time to experience whatever feelings and thoughts come up in association with this deep purpose, and write about them. . . .

If you have any images or nonverbal impressions of this deep purpose, see if you can capture them in a drawing. . . . [3]

A Powerful Technique

This exercise can be used with any projects or problems in your life. For example, you might start with the question "What is my purpose in redecorating my living room?" If you respond, "To make it look nicer," you would then ask, "What is my purpose in making the living room look nicer?" And so on. You might ask, "What is my purpose in wanting to change my son's behavior?" or "What is my purpose in participating in a demonstration?" and see where you go. This is a powerful technique for discovering what is really important to you and why. In some cases, you may discover you have no real purpose in doing something or that the purpose is in conflict with other values and directions.

Carry your deep sense of purpose with you for the next few weeks. Give it time to expand, become clearer, and even change in response to the realities of your life. We will refer to it in future sections of the book.

AN IDEAL MODEL

We carry around many images or models of ourselves, consciously and unconsciously. Many of these images are based on things others have said or what we thought was said, often in moments of anger or confusion. So we may have images of ourselves as inadequate, stupid, or ugly because other children taunted us with such labels when we were young. Or our parents may have said disparaging things to us out of their own inadequacy and frustration. Often these inferior images and models are reinforced by our partners and spouses, who fight back when they feel put down or threatened in some way. We have many opportunities to develop inferior models for ourselves, and unless we are fortunate, few chances to develop positive ones.

We may also carry within us models and images that we have created in reaction to the destructive ones foisted on us by an unsympathetic world. These images might be like those in *The Secret Life of Walter Mitty,* by James Thurber.[4] Walter Mitty is a mousey fellow with a domineering wife; he compensates by constantly daydreaming about himself performing heroically in various crises. Most of us wouldn't go as far as Walter, but we may create unrealistic, unattainable expectations that contribute to our sense of inadequacy when we fall short.

So in setting our sights, we may need to sort through these various self-images and models. By making them conscious, we can adapt them to the realities of our strengths and circumstances. No longer subverting our self-esteem or distracting us with daydreams, our self-images and models can strengthen and empower us. We can bring the best qualities of these images together in a realistic and inspiring "ideal model." It will not be an ultimate model of perfection but, rather, will represent the next major stage in our unfolding life path. We can modify and expand it as we grow along.

The next exercise will help you sort out the various models you hold and help you find beneath them a unifying "ideal model." The exercise includes five drawings (so have drawing materials available) and takes at least a half hour to complete.[5] Remember that we use drawings to move beyond the rational mind and tap into the unconscious.

∞

Ideal Model Exercise

Sit now in a relaxed position and pay attention to your breathing. Allow your breathing to settle into a deep rhythm. . . . Allow your feelings to become calm and your mind to quiet. Move to a place of safety and peace within yourself. . . .

You will be asking yourself a series of questions. After each one, allow a picture, body sensation, or sound to emerge to represent your response. When you feel ready, make a drawing of this image. Take as much time as you need. When your drawing is complete, make some notes below it about your feelings and thoughts. Then close your eyes and return to the peaceful, safe place within. Allow your breathing to quiet your feelings and thoughts before you read the next question.

1.

All of us underevaluate ourselves in some way. We have an image or model of ourselves that is worse than we really are. Sometimes we believe this model to be true. Ask yourself now, *What model, worse than I really am, do I carry of myself?*

2.

We also overevaluate ourselves in some ways. We have images of ourselves that are better than we really are, and we sometimes believe these images are the whole truth. Ask yourself now, *What model, better than I really am, do I carry of myself?*

3.

We tend to hold "secret daydreams" for ourselves, images of how we think we'd like to be in a fantasy world. Ask yourself now, *What is an unrealistic daydream image I have of myself, a model that I know I can never realize?* Although this image may have some appeal to you, it probably lacks vitality because it is so unreal. . . .

4.

Now ask yourself, *How would other people like me to be? What do others expect of me, or how would they like me to change?* You may want to think of a general "others" for this or focus on a few important relationships. . . .

Now stand up and with your eyes closed, get in touch with the weight of all these images and models. . . . Feel how they limit and restrict you, how they hold you down. . . . Actively shake off these images now! Shake them off and let the weight and restriction drop off you with an act of will. . . . Let go of them. . . .

Now stand quietly for a while, experiencing how you feel. . . .

5.

Sit down again, close your eyes, and center yourself again. Allow your breath to calm and deepen. . . . Then consider what you really and realistically would like to become. Ask yourself, *How do I really want to be?* Let an image emerge for this model from deep within you. . . . Take time for this, trusting what comes, and becoming more familiar with it. . . . Add to it any other qualities you think appropriate, and allow anything undesirable to drop away. . . .

When you are ready, open your eyes and draw your image, your ideal model. . . . Take time to create a drawing that represents your inner experience. Make notes about your feelings and thoughts too. . . .

Close your eyes again, and holding the image and the feelings of your ideal model in your mind, allow your breath to become slower and deeper, relaxing your body. . . .

Now imagine that you can step right into this image, you can become this model. Let yourself really take on the qualities of this ideal as if you had already grown in these ways. . . .

If you feel comfortable doing so, stand up and move around, experiencing what it is like to embody your ideal model. . . . What are your posture and movements like? What expression do you sense on your face? . . . Write about your experience of being your ideal model. . . .

FEELINGS AND CONFLICTS

As you continue to think about and visualize your ideal model, your sense of purpose, and your image of your next step, you may find feelings and conflicts coming to the surface. Sometimes in your visualizations of your ideal model, the opposite qualities may emerge. If you are imagining yourself speaking with confidence to an audience, for example, you may experience more anxiety and find yourself imagining the audience ignoring or heckling you.

The unconscious feelings and blocks that have been quietly holding you back all along are coming to the surface because you are challenging their control. You can now be aware of them and begin to work through them. This does not mean that your ideal model is wrong or that you can never realize it. Actually, these resistances are only making themselves known because you are on the brink of change. They are fighting their last battle, so to speak.

As you will see in the next chapter, we do not reject or eliminate these blocks. We could not, even if we tried. Instead we explore them for their hidden gifts to us and bring them along as partners in our intended changes. For now, however, simply notice what comes up as you set your sights and dream your dreams and then gently reaffirm your choices.

6. *Working with Blocks in Our Path*

*N*OW LET'S TALK ABOUT THE HANG-UPS. We knew we'd have to deal with them sooner or later. It may have seemed, however, with all this work on acceptance, centering, potential, and ideal models, that we would try to simply transcend our problems or blithely go along as if they didn't exist. The power of positive thinking, and all that.

Actually, what we have done is laid the foundations for more successful work with our hang-ups and blocks. Rather than burrowing into our problems first, as we sometimes tend to do, we have created a context in which exploring the less desirable parts of ourselves will be far easier. We have a stronger sense of the inner resources we can call upon. We have a clearer sense of direction, or where we are going, which will help motivate us to take care of whatever is in our way. And rather than looking at our every little imperfection, we need only confront those that actually are getting in our way at any given time.

So if you are ready, let's begin this exploration. It may be enjoyable at times, painful at other times, difficult at first, then surprisingly easy. Let's start with another in the series of questions-drawings we have been using. In chapter 5, you explored the question of your next step in life, what is emerging and possible now in your life. You also developed an "ideal model."

Look back in your journal and drawings to refresh your memory of those visions before going on to this next question.

∽

What Is Getting in My Way?

Have ready a sheet of paper or a page in your journal, and drawing materials. Sit in a comfortable upright position and close your eyes. Take a few moments to simply breathe, allowing your body to come to rest. . . .

Now quietly observe your feelings and thoughts. Notice any fear or excitement you may be experiencing. Notice ideas and questions you have about this exercise. Let these feelings and thoughts be there, and let them also come to rest. . . .

Move toward that quiet, safe place inside where you can be open, receptive, and patient, where you can receive responses from within. . . .

Recall now your sense of potential, your purpose, and your ideal model. Gently holding those images and ideas, ask yourself: *What gets in the way of moving toward my next step? What holds me back?* Allow images, sensations, feelings, and thoughts to arise in response to these questions. Observe them. . . .

When you feel ready, open your eyes and find a way of capturing your responses in a drawing, and then make notes about your feelings and thoughts. . . .[1]

∽

Compare this drawing to the ones you did in chapters 2 and 5, on "Where am I now in my life?" and "What is possible for me in my life?" Notice any common themes or images. You might share this drawing with someone to further explore its implications.

Notice especially your feelings toward this drawing. Do you feel satisfied at having gotten some inner secrets out on paper? Do you feel frightened or repulsed by the images? Are you amused? The Identification Exercise from chapter 3 may be very useful at this point to help you accept your images and your feelings about them.

Your drawing may be a representation of a part or parts of yourself that seem to have a life of their own. You may feel as if you have little demons inside you that get in your way. These demons seem separate from you, somewhat alien, although all too familiar. In psychosynthesis, these semi-autonomous parts of ourselves are called "subpersonalities."

SUBPERSONALITIES: THE MANY FACES OF EVERYONE

One of the most liberating discoveries of my life was learning that it is okay to be more ways than one. It is not a sign of mental instability that I act and feel radically different ways at different times. If anything, it is a sign of health. I have more than one way of responding to life's challenges, more than one way of coping. If one doesn't work, I can try another. If being sweet doesn't help, I can get tough. I can even experience two seemingly conflicting points of view within myself at the same time. I can be both frightened and assertive; I can be both angry and caring. This discovery gives me a sense of flexibility and freedom that I continue to enjoy, especially when I remember my previous belief about how I was "supposed" to be.

Our various ways of being and acting are often crystallized into behavior patterns, or "subpersonalities." Because being sweet is often useful, for example, we develop a sweet little girl or boy subpersonality. Our sense of identity gets temporarily attached to that way of being, and we think that is all we are.

For a period of time, we think and feel and act as if being sweet were the only option available to us. We become trapped in a worldview (the world is threatening and I must be sweet to avoid punishment) and a personal identification (I am someone who is always sweet, never grouchy), both of which limit our freedom.

Sometimes, It's a Matter of Survival

Subpersonalities form out of challenging life situations, often in childhood. We discover that a certain set of attitudes and behaviors seem to help us survive a challenging or threatening situation, and we learn the habit of reacting in that way. It serves us to do so; it helps us survive emotionally, sometimes even physically. Our ingenuity in creating subpersonalities is often quite astonishing. Children can survive the most horrendous situations through skillfully created subpersonalities.

Because this process is largely unconscious, however, we tend to generalize these patterns of attitude and behavior into other life situations as we grow into adulthood. A scowl on the face of a stranger may unconsciously remind us of an angry father and suddenly, without knowing why, we are feeling and acting out of the defensive subpersonality we developed as a child. This subpersonality may be entirely inappropriate for the immediate circumstance; it may actually disempower us rather than help us survive. Unfortunately, while we are caught up in those feelings, we cannot see any other options for ourselves, for we really are like the helpless child again, acting the only way we know how.

Subpersonalities are habitual ways of reacting to circumstances, habits that often create even more problems. We learn these habits from others as well as creating them for ourselves. Codependency, a whole collection of habitual responses to living in a dysfunctional family, is a common sub-personality pattern. Children can learn it from a parent. I believe I learned many of my codependent habits from imitating my mother, who in turn was well trained in that tradition by her own family and the culture in which she was raised.

Nations May Have Subpersonalities

Yes, we have cultural subpersonalities as well as individual ones. We can even see a whole nation becoming caught up in a subpersonality, with its limited view of reality and limited arena for response. Wars may result from this kind of collective identification. All too often, United States military actions abroad result from political leaders and citizens alike becoming enmeshed in an overly defensive, belligerent collective subpersonality. And each of us who becomes so enmeshed is responding from his or her own personal version of that subpersonality.

The military example is appropriate because it is helpful to think of subpersonalities as loyal soldiers following orders issued long ago in a war that has long since ended. They continue to fight the battle for our survival when our survival is no longer in doubt. They are like the Japanese soldier who was discovered on a remote Pacific island years after the end of World War II. The soldier didn't know the war was over and had maintained his fortified post faithfully, prepared for any attack. He was hailed as a hero and brought home with full military honors because he had remained faithful to his orders, even though they were long obsolete.

The following exercise can help you become aware of and work with one of your loyal soldiers. After you read each set of instructions, close your eyes and take some time inside before you write about your responses. This is a meditative imagery and writing process which is best done at a leisurely pace.

∞

Seeking a Loyal Soldier

Take a few minutes to find a relaxed and comfortable position. Close your eyes and just be aware of your breathing. . . .

Now begin to review your daily life over the past few weeks. Start with today and move backward until you find a time or times when you felt afraid or anxious or constricted in some way. Perhaps it was about money, or a relationship, or your job, or some other aspect of your life. Choose a time when you were not in any immediate physical danger. . . .

Allow yourself to relive this experience. Recall your feelings, your thoughts, your physical sensations and responses. . . . How does the world look from here? . . . How do you feel about your own abilities? . . . What actions are you tempted to take? . . .

Now, in your imagination, step away from yourself in the situation you have just recalled. See yourself as someone else looking at the situation might see you, someone able to perceive all the feelings, thoughts, and reactions you experience. Observe without judgement, just seeing who is there, what subpersonality is reacting to this situation. . . .

Notice what this subpersonality is trying to do for you. Ask it what it is trying to do and really listen to what it has to say. . . .

Find a way to communicate your appreciation for its loyal service to you. Let this subpersonality know you are grateful for its attempts to take care of you. . . .

Now consider how this subpersonality limits you when it's in charge. Notice its blinders, its limiting beliefs about you or the world. . . .

Perhaps you can sense what it really needs, what qualities or energies it needs to be more effective for you. . . .

Are you willing to give it what it needs? Imagine doing so symbolically. Notice how it responds. . . .

Take a few moments now to make any agreements you might need to better integrate this loyal soldier into your personality. . . . Then find a way to say good-bye to this sub-personality for now. Write about the whole experience and about the feelings and thoughts that you have now.

ॐ

A process like this can be very emotional. The combined relief and pain of reclaiming and caring for a "lost" part of one-self is often enormous. If this is the case for you, take the time you need to allow these feelings to run their course before moving on. Practice a centering technique from chapter 3. Write about your changing feelings in your journal.

Self-observation and disidentification, which we have prac-ticed in previous chapters, help us become aware of our sub-personalities. Once the reaction pattern is conscious, it is far easier to change. Awareness is only the first step, however, because this more or less alienated part of oneself needs to be brought back into the fold. Although our first impulse may be to just get rid of the troublesome part, this is not the way to wholeness and wouldn't work anyway. The qualities and skills of every subpersonality are too much a part of us to be aban-doned and are of too much value to be scorned. Instead, we work to transform and reintegrate these important parts of ourselves.

Befriending a Subpersonality

To become better acquainted, we may, for a time, treat the subpersonality almost as if it were a separate person or creature we wanted to befriend. From a centered place of compassion, we discover what is missing in the subpersonality, what qualities, perspectives, or life experiences it lacks. We make a commitment to meet its needs—for love, courage and strength, humility, or perspective and discipline. Usually its needs are for a quality we have available to us in another part of our personality or which we can readily develop. Sometimes we may ask for support or guidance from trusted family members or professionals; this, too, is a way of taking responsibility for ourselves. From center, we can draw upon all our resources, inner and outer, to meet our legitimate subpersonality needs.

We also acknowledge what the subpersonality is trying to do for us, what qualities and skills it has to offer us. We come to a new agreement with the subpersonality about its role in our life, so we can draw upon it as a resource in meeting various life challenges.

The next exercise is a similar process, this time working with the image you drew in the exercise "What is getting in my way?" If you drew more than one, you can work with the one that seems to have the most emotional impact or see if all your images seem to come from the same place in yourself. This process needs your undivided attention, so, if possible, work in a private place and allow yourself at least fifteen minutes.

∞

Subpersonality Dialogue

Take a few moments to center yourself, breathing, relaxing, bringing your awareness into yourself. . . . Then recall your imagery in response to the question *What's getting in my way? What's holding me back?* Looking at your drawing may help. You will be holding a conversation with this part of yourself, between this part of yourself and you as Observer.

Focus your attention on this image and imagine *becoming* it. How does it feel to be this part of yourself? Really let yourself experience this part of you from the inside. . . .

Begin to write about how you feel as this part and what you want from the other parts of yourself or from life in general. Don't hold anything back; just let it all come out, willy-nilly. . . .

When you've said all you want to say as the part, imagine that you can step into a more centered and whole perspective, into your Observer. Read over what the part has said; really pay attention and take it all in. . . .

Now respond to what the first subpersonality has written. Write how you feel about it, how it is affecting your life and, from a compassionate perspective, what you understand about its predicament. . . .

If it has something to say in response, write its words and pay attention to them. Move back and forth between these two points of view, the subpersonality and the Observer, as you write the dialogue that unfolds. . . .

Begin to explore in your dialogue the following questions:

What does this part most deeply need to be whole?

Are you willing to give this part what it needs? How might you go about doing this?

How would the subpersonality feel about receiving this gift? How might the gift transform it?

What has this part been trying to do for you all these years?

What does the part have to offer? What is the quality, skill, or wisdom it can bring to your whole person? As the centered one, be sure to acknowledge this. Be gracious; write about how you value its gift, how you need it in your life.

How can you work together more harmoniously in the future so that its gift is used effectively and its needs are met?

When you feel ready to finish your dialogue, close your eyes for a moment and refocus on your image of this part of yourself. Notice if it has changed. See if either of you has anything more to say. . . . Then make some general notes on what you learned through this experience.[2]

◌

PRECIOUS QUALITIES

Working with subpersonalities is one of the most powerful means for personal and spiritual growth. Subpersonalities hold our most precious qualities bound up in their crystallized forms. When we discover what they have to offer, and when we meet their needs, they become resources rather than blocks. My colleague Walter Polt says, "The part of you which you hate and fear the most holds the key to your salvation." The demoralizing "Critic" subpersonality may have the qualities of discernment and discipline. A "Helpless Child" subpersonality may hold the qualities of vulnerability, humility, and interdependence.

Picture a superconscious quality as a precious gem coming from the superconscious, seeking expression in the personality. The circumstances around the personality (family and social norms and dysfunctional patterns) do not allow this gem to shine freely. Mud is thrown at it and it gets buried. Gradually the mud hardens and the gem sinks lower into the lower unconscious, weighed down by fear and confusion. But then someone comes digging, bringing the chunk of mud up into the light of day. Perhaps it is washed gently in a stream, or the solidified mud is broken away. The gem reappears and is welcomed. Now it is able to shine in its true form.

Perhaps you have found the precious gem at the heart of what was getting in your way. If not, you may want to repeat the process at another time. Or you may wait and see what comes to you spontaneously in the next few days. When the earth is very hard, we have to soak it awhile before we can dig. Perhaps the gem will wash to the surface on its own.

We have numerous subpersonalities, some buried more deeply than others. Use this exercise whenever you encounter a block, a difficult feeling or state of mind. In time the process may become second nature so that you can pause in your activities and seek out who and what are temporarily running the show, what they need, and what their gift and truth might be. You may be able to do this within a few minutes. But you may need to go through a more structured process when you encounter a particularly entrenched old soldier who won't easily give up his or her post.

WARRING PAIRS

Subpersonalities often come in warring pairs. For every "Oppressor," there is probably a "Victim" or a "Rebel" or both. When we "disidentify" from one subpersonality, we may find ourselves identified with another conflicting one. The clues are in our feelings and thoughts: feelings of dislike, rejection, fear, and anger. Thoughts of criticism and judgement may signal that we are not really "in center." From center, we usually feel somewhat detached, yet very caring and compassionate; we feel both concerned and capable of handling whatever challenges come.

When two or more subpersonalities appear, we need to move into center all the more strongly and act as a mediator among them. We may ask them to take turns and discuss their needs and gifts one at a time. We may imagine helping them communicate with each other. Sometimes it is helpful to take them into the presence of the Wise Being and ask for guidance. The next exercise provides an opportunity for you to do that using a process similar to that in chapter 4, page 61. Before you begin, take a few moments to decide which two conflicting subpersonalities you want to use. You may experience them as two arguing voices within you that keep you from knowing what to do. Or you may be aware of them as distinct images or aspects of yourself. If you are not in touch with two such conflicting parts right now, you may want to skip this exercise and come back to it when you need it.

∽

Journey to the Wise Being

As usual, take a few moments to relax and pay attention to your breathing. Bring your attention within yourself, letting the outside world go for now. Breathe. . . .

Now imagine yourself in a meadow surrounded by woods and mountains. The sun is shining and it is a beautiful day. Enjoy the meadow, its sights, sounds, and smells. . . .

If they are not already present, bring your two conflicting subpersonalities into the meadow with you. You may want to keep one on either side of you. See and feel them with you, and notice what you feel about having them there. . . .

You are about to take a short journey with these two parts of yourself, a journey to see the Wise Being. Make whatever arrangements you need to bring these two parts along with you comfortably. Then look around and find a trail leading into the woods and up the slope of a mountain nearby. . . .

Begin to walk along the trail, noticing the sights and sounds around you. Notice how your two friends journey along with you. Notice what is easy and what is difficult about walking up this trail.

The trail now slopes upward and begins to climb the mountainside. Take your time. . . .

Soon you are already about a third of the way to the top. . . .

Now you are halfway up. . . .

Now you can see the top not far above you. . . . Take a few minutes to complete your climb to the top of the mountain, resting for a while if you arrive before the next suggestion. . . .

Look around and enjoy the view. Let the sun warm you or the breeze cool you so that you are quite comfortable. Notice how your companions are doing. . . .

As you rest, you see the figure coming toward you through the sunlight. At it comes into view, you see that it is a very Wise and Loving Being. Its face and eyes convey love and wisdom as the figure approaches. Let yourself take in the love. . . .

When you feel ready, talk to this Wise and Loving Being about your two companions. Tell about the conflict they are in and about your struggle to reconcile these two parts of yourself. . . . Ask for insight and guidance. . . .

Receive whatever communication the Wise Being offers, verbally or silently. The Wise Being may touch each of you, blessing you with whatever each part needs. . . . Notice how each of your companions responds to the Wise Being . . .

Take time to complete your visit together. . . . When you feel ready, return down the trail to the meadow with your companions in whatever form they now appear. . . .

Bring them back with you into the room where you are sitting. Become aware of the sounds of the room around you, of your body and your breathing. . . .

When you are ready, write about your experience in the meadow, on the trail, and at the top of the mountain with the Wise Being. Be sure to note any images or events that happened unexpectedly. Note what was easy and what was difficult. What guidance did the Wise Being offer? How did your subpersonalities change, if at all?

⌒

Strong and Useful Alliances

Often when two subpersonalities are in conflict, each has just the quality that the other needs. Many of us would recognize an inner conflict between a judgemental "Critic" subpersonality and another part that feels like a "Stupid Kid." The more the Critic rails about our failings, the more stupid the Kid feels, thereby goading the Critic into louder action. In working with these two, we might discover that the Critic has discernment, which the Stupid Kid needs, while the Kid has humility, which is what the Critic lacks. The Wise Being may help them to cooperate with one another and to transform into more harmonious forms. Strong and useful alliances can often be built between previously warring subpersonalities through compassionate mediation by the centered self.

When we make peace with our own parts, we are contributing in a subtle but effective way to peace in our families, communities, and world. I am far less likely to get caught up in an unthinking collective reaction, a collective subpersonality, if I have recognized, accepted, and integrated the corresponding parts of myself. Fascist movements such as that which occurred in Nazi Germany, for example, result from each participant's unconsciously identifying with an authoritarian subpersonality within himself or herself. Yet, most participants would hotly deny having or acting from such a self-image.

Acceptance, inclusion, and integration are the keys to wholeness. No part of us, no matter how repugnant, gets thrown out. Every aspect has value and truth. As soon as we reject or deny any part of ourselves, we are fragmented. Wholeness means exactly that: no part left out. And that is easier said than done. Fear and prejudice cause just as much alienation within ourselves as they cause in our social relations.

In the next chapter, we will take on some demons that are very difficult to accept: anger, fear, depression, shame, and addiction. Somehow we must find ways of including these energies, for they too have gifts for us; they too are part of our wholeness.

7. *Transforming the Demons Within*

*F*EELINGS SUCH AS ANGER AND FEAR bring up complex issues and reactions in most of us. To some extent, our social conditioning around these feelings is gender-based: women aren't supposed to get mad, and men aren't supposed to be afraid. So sometimes when men get frightened, they feel angry; when women get angry, they may feel afraid. Confusing, isn't it? It is not always easy to know what we're feeling, much less transform those feelings into something positive for ourselves. Better just to bury them and put on a happy face. Or storm around, let off steam, and then get back to "normal."

To add to our difficulties, as children we may have modeled ourselves after the adults around us by either taking on or reacting against their behavior patterns. If one of our parents expressed anger through violence, for example, we may also have developed a tendency toward violence. Or we may have gone to the opposite extreme, acting very meek in the most provoking situations. If one of our parents acted like a victim, trying to placate a domineering partner, we may have also played the victim/martyr. Or we may have reacted against this role by being especially aggressive and quick to counterattack at the slightest hint of conflict. We may have developed distinct subpersonalities around these reactions.

Similarly, we may overexpress or repress other strong feelings, such as grief, hurt, shame, and disappointment. We may repress feelings of despair brought on by the threat of nuclear war or environmental catastrophe. We sense that it would be socially unacceptable to talk about our despair with others. ("What a bummer! Can't you talk about something more cheerful?") Our unconscious and unexpressed feelings may drive us into abuse of alcohol and other drugs, into eating disorders, into sexual and "love" addictions, and into unhealthy relationships.

Many excellent books and self-help groups exist today to support recovery from addictions and dysfunctional family patterns. Many also help people cope with anger and grief. Here we will focus on what psychosynthesis theory and practice have to offer us in dealing with these inner "demons" as part of our journey to wholeness. Readers who want to explore any of these issues in more depth may refer to the bibliography at the end of the book for ideas about where to go next.

ANGER

Anger often covers fear and may be a more accessible feeling for many of us, so we'll explore it first. To begin, reflect on your own attitudes and assumptions about anger, using the questions at the top of page 93 to guide this process for you. Notice the layers of attitudes and beliefs you have: how do you think you ought to feel and how do you really feel? Are there secret assumptions buried underneath your more rational ideas?

∞

Reflections on Anger

What makes you angry? How do you deal with anger? Do you get angry easily or rarely? Do you recover quickly, or do you stay angry a long time? What do you do when you're angry?

How do you react when others are angry about something? What if they are angry with you?

What beliefs and values do you hold about anger? How would you like to change your relationship with anger?

∞

Walter Polt has developed a powerful process for transforming anger into power. This process recognizes the basic validity of our anger: anger comes up in response to a perceived threat to our well-being and integrity. When we discover what we are protecting and affirm it consciously and actively, our anger becomes constructive. We can sort out real threats from imagined ones and take appropriate action. Walter Polt generously wrote up the following exercise and comments especially for inclusion here.

∞

The Anger to Power Process

In preparation for this exercise, think of someone in your life whose actions bother you, and pick one behavior you dislike. If several issues are annoying you, it is important to guard against becoming overwhelmed and hopeless. So mentally list all these issues, and then choose one to focus on for now.

Now express the fact of the behavior you have chosen in a simple statement, like "Joe often comes late." If your statement is a judgement ("He's a jerk"), an interpretation ("He's selfish"), or a generalization ("He's always late"), restate it objectively, the way a camera would see it. Write down an objective statement of the behavior.

Now take some time to relax and allow yourself to breathe easily. . . . Notice any physical tension, and imagine you're breathing softly into the tense places as you allow your body to relax. . . . Note some of the emotions you're feeling and let them subside. . . . What are you thinking? Observe the thoughts. . . . Let them go, and focus on your easy breathing. . . .

PHASE 1

Now recall the offensive behavior named in your objective statement. Formulate a statement (addressed to the person) that sums up clearly what the person did or is doing: "What you did (or are doing) is this: _____." Write it down.

Perhaps you're aware of unfortunate consequences resulting from the person's behavior. Allow yourself to feel some of your painful memories and emotions about the behavior. . . . Acknowledge the damage it causes. . . .

Repeat your statement a few times and notice your feelings and thoughts. . . . What are you learning as you review how much you dislike this behavior?

Where in your body do you feel your feelings about this? Allow yourself to feel your dislike, but not so much your dislike of the person as of the behavior. Experience it in your mind, emotions, and body. . . .

PHASE 2

Now ask yourself, *What would I prefer that this person do?* It's good to notice and write down all of your preferences, even if they seem absurd or impossible to fulfill.

Now select one thing that you especially prefer that the person do. . . . State your preferred behavior clearly: "A behavior I'd prefer from you in place of what you did (are doing) is this: ____."

State your preference aloud to yourself and notice the feelings and images that come up. . . . If you imagine good things happening, enjoy the fantasy. . . .

As you continue to state your preference to yourself, do you feel longing? Let yourself feel this longing. . . . Do you feel conviction and strength? Allow yourself the excitement they bring you. . . . Before going on to the next step, make some notes about any feelings and thoughts you have about your preference.

PHASE 3

Take a few moments to quiet your feelings and thoughts. Notice where your selected preference seems to come from inside you. Some very personal belief or value of yours is at the base of it. . . .

Begin to identify this belief or value, since it is something you consider important. It will be something important not only for you but also for the whole world. . . . Write a clear statement of this value, like this: "I believe in ____" or "I believe things generally go better for people when they ____."

State your belief or value aloud and notice how you feel saying this. . . . Does your breathing change? Does your posture or your sense of well-being change? As you state your belief, perhaps images or memories come to you. Enjoy them. . . . Maybe you can see where this value comes from in your past or current experience. . . . If you feel gratitude for this, enjoy the feeling. Notice how your gratitude heals you. . . .

Imagine what your life would be like if you didn't hold this value. . . . Consider how hard (even impossible) it would be to give up this belief. It is part of your identity. It is an aspect or quality of your very Self. . . . Affirm this to yourself by saying and writing: "My belief in ____ is part of who I am. I intend to live my life according to this value."

Allow an image to come for this quality. . . . Can you become this image, identify with it? Imagine the source of the image . . . and be the source. . . .

Take time to enjoy the experience. . . . When you feel ready, draw your image and write about your impressions and feelings.

∞

Inner Work and Outer Work

You can look at your experience of this exercise as "inner work" for your own personal benefit. "Outer work" might include communicating with the person toward whom you've been feeling angry. If you feel it is appropriate to say something, choose your style and setting thoughtfully: do you want to communicate by letter, phone, or face-to-face? Will the two of you be alone or with a third party? Choose your statements creatively; a quiet start is sometimes more effective than "big guns." Allow time for, and really listen to, the other person's response. Make room for honest interaction.

If the person with whom you have been angry is not available to you, or if you decide no useful purpose will be served by talking directly with him or her, you can still practice expressing your anger in a positive, empowering way. Write a letter to the person, telling him or her what behavior you dislike and how it has affected your life and well-being. Tell the person what behavior you would prefer and the value or belief upon which your preference is based. You can keep this letter in your journal or burn it ceremonially. You can also have a conversation aloud by imagining the person sitting before you in a chair, or by asking a friend or counselor to role-play the other person for you.

You may want to repeat this exercise several times, focusing on other behaviors that anger you. In time, it may become almost second nature to respond in this way to frustrating or hurtful interactions with others. You may find yourself identifying the other person's behavior objectively, in a way that does not attack or insult, and following that by stating your preference and affirming your values.

Forgiveness often follows a process like this, as we let go of our demands that others conform to our values and choices. Forgiveness doesn't mean, however, that we will tolerate repetitions of the disliked behavior. We may make choices about our future interaction with the other person to prevent repetition. Forgiveness is an important final step in the anger-to-power process.

FEAR

Fear may be our most primal emotion and is based on our basic drive to survive. We experience fear when something threatens our survival and we are motivated to save ourselves. It's a very practical emotion! So what's the problem?

My problem is that I am often afraid when there is no real danger, and such fear limits me in very tangible ways. I am afraid of making Mistakes as if every mistake were life-threatening, when in fact few are. But that fear sometimes makes me conservative in my speech and actions, keeps me from trying out new ideas. Fear keeps me stuck. It may even cause me to run away from situations that could be beneficial. It might cause me to run smack into real danger in the process of fleeing an imagined one.

Fear can paralyze my mind as my body goes into "fight-or-flight" mode. An aggressive, hostile response from someone else scares the wits out of me, and I forget what I know to be true. Later, I will probably think of several reasonable arguments I could have made, but at the time I go blank. This kind of fear is not practical, although it comes to defend me. I need to move beyond; I need to disidentify from it. Then the fear can be a clue that hostile energy may indeed be coming toward me, even though it may be couched in "reasonable" words. In recognizing the hostility, I also can discern the fear in the other person's heart. I can respond to the other's fear with greater compassion and wisdom because I am freed from reflexive self-defense.

Denying Fear

Perhaps what is most damaging is when fear is so great that I think I cannot cope with it, so I make it unconscious. I deny that the fear exists, and usually the fearful situation as well. I escape, go numb, space out. Then two things happen: I am unable to do anything about the fearful situation, which may in fact be truly threatening, and my repressed fear finds expression in some other, covert way. I may become ill or inappropriately frightened about something quite separate and harmless.

The threat of nuclear war, which reached a peak in the eighties with an apparently unstoppable arms race between the United States and the former Soviet Union, aroused fear in everyone. The prospect of global annihilation was too much for most of us to take. Collectively, we went numb. We became absorbed in short-term gratification and material gain, trying to escape from the horror. Obviously this failed to solve the very real problem of runaway arms development, and as a society we were sickened by our denial. Our values and priorities were distorted by our repressed fear.

I want to continue to feel fear, just not be consumed by it. I want to know when I am threatened, on any level, so I can respond appropriately. Just because I feel afraid doesn't necessarily mean there is anything to be afraid of. Nevertheless, it is always worth checking out. If I deny or suppress my feelings of fear, I may miss some important information. The challenge is to feel it without identifying with it.

What are some of the fears you carry with you day to day? They may seem huge, or they may seem insignificant, but still you know they limit you in various ways. Perhaps you are afraid of what other people think or of making Mistakes (as I fear). Perhaps you are afraid of taking a risk in a relationship or in your job. Perhaps you are afraid to tell a difficult truth or have a physical symptom checked out by a doctor. Take a few minutes to consider what some of your personal fears are, and then choose one for the process that follows—a method to sort out the beliefs and assumptions beneath your fear and discover a deeper truth. Choose a manageable fear for trying out the process.

∞

What Am I Afraid Of?

Take a few moments to relax and pay attention to your breathing. Bring your attention within yourself, letting the outside world go for now. Breathe. . . .

Consider what makes you afraid in your life and the one fear you have chosen for this exercise. State it clearly: "I am afraid of . . ."

Let yourself experience your fear. How does it affect your body, your breathing, your muscle tension? How does your mind react to the fear? What other feelings come up? Now ask yourself what would happen if what you fear came to pass. What are you afraid would happen next if what you fear actually occurred?

And if that happened, what are you afraid would happen next? What might happen to you?

And if that happened, what are you afraid would happen next?

Continue in this way, writing each time you respond. Explore the fear behind the fear, working through the levels until you reach what seems to be the most basic fear.

Now notice your feelings, your thoughts, and your physical responses to this most basic fear. Remember to breathe. . . .

Imagine moving into a very deep and centered place in yourself, where you are in touch with your fear but not consumed by it. . . .

Now, what truth do you know about all this? What is your deepest, truest knowing?

You may or may not be able to put this deep truth in words, but you can feel it in your soul. Let it move into your body. Breathe it into your tissues. . . .

When you are ready, write about this truth. Draw an image of it if you wish, or create a poem or song about it. Affirm this truth while experiencing your fear.[1]

An Awareness of Deeper Truth

As with so many of our reactions to life, we may need only to become aware of how fear works within us and the beliefs or assumptions on which it is based. This awareness allows us to step back and see a larger reality, a deeper truth. Fears are often based on our experiences as relatively helpless children, who we no longer are. We have acquired much wisdom, skill, and power upon which we can draw. Many of our fears have not caught up with this fact!

Sometimes, on the other hand, we look at the basis of our fears and discover that, yes, indeed, there is a real threat here! Our livelihood may be in real danger, our immediate physical safety may be in peril, or we may be facing one of the very real threats to the continuation of human existence on the planet. But we have already stepped back, centered ourselves a bit, and are therefore in a much better position to take defensive, protective action. We are less likely to be paralyzed, and more likely to act positively and effectively. And we may be able to reduce the stress on our physical bodies, which want either to fight or to flee; neither reaction is usually appropriate in our world today.

UP AGAINST THE MYSTERY

Something that causes me a lot of anxiety (another word for fear) is not knowing what is going on, or what will happen next, or what I should be prepared to do. When I have a pain in my body and I don't know "the cause," I get frightened. I want an explanation about it. Once I "understand," I relax and the pain is lessened. I can accept the pain much more readily, even if I can't do anything about it. If the pain is not severe, I can even go on with my ordinary routine.

There's something terrifying about not knowing. When I work with a client in counseling, I like to have a sense of what needs to happen and how I can facilitate that process. When a client is really stuck, however, I often feel stuck too. Then I feel afraid that I am not doing my job, that I am inadequate, even a phony. My self-image is challenged. I also want very much to help the other person because I see his or her pain, and if I don't know what to do, we just have to sit in the pain together.

If I have a theory that applies to the situation, or better yet, a technique I think will work, my fear is relieved. I feel competent and able to help. My client may feel better too, at least in the moment, because someone is taking care of the situation.

Not Knowing Is Scary

There's something terrifying about not knowing. Many of us are becoming painfully aware of the enormous problems facing the human race today: problems of conflict, oppression, and the environment. We see a world poised on the brink of ecological and human disaster, and nothing we do seems to make that much difference. What works, works slowly, and with unexpected complications. Our world is at risk and we don't know what to do. So many of us choose what seems to be a manageable task, a problem we think we know how to solve, and try to ignore the rest.

When we are terrified about not knowing, we reach for certainty, we reach for formulas. When I am in pain and don't know why, I consult a physician, an outside authority who knows about bodies and who will tell me what to do, such as take a medication. As a counselor, I reach into my bag of tricks; I recall something I was taught in my training, or have read about, or have observed in someone else's work. I try to remember how I'm "supposed" to handle this kind of situation. When I feel concern about a global problem, I read what various experts and authorities have to say—the more definitely and confidently they write, the better.

But so much of our knowledge today contradicts yesterday's! How much will today's knowledge be contradicted tomorrow? We know from experience within our own lifetime that "knowledge" changes, sometimes flip-flops. I was raised on the "expert" advice that we need lots of protein, which meant meat every day. Now many nutritionists are saying we consume far too much protein; instead, we need complex carbohydrates. I have become a vegetarian and find I do quite well without the nutritional god of meat of my childhood. Apparently, we cannot really rely on outside authority, expert advice, or common knowledge. So we're back in the fear of not knowing again!

In the previous chapter, we explored the idea of subpersonalities, those semiautonomous patterns of behavior, feelings, and thought that sometimes take over our whole sense of who we are. Many of our subpersonalities may be threatened by our lack of certain knowledge and start demanding our attention; they may even temporarily take charge. When I am in physical pain, I may become a "Frightened Child," looking to Mommy to make it all better. In a counseling situation, my "Competent Therapist" subpersonality may react because her very identity is called into question by "not knowing." If she doesn't know, then she must not be competent anymore, and then what?

These subpersonalities are often out of touch with the larger reality of our lives and our inner and outer resources. From their point of view, there truly is danger in not knowing. From our center, we can feel confident in our ability to take care of whatever occurs, without advance knowledge. We know we have available a vast array of wisdom, skill, intuition, power, discernment, and love to respond to whatever difficulties and dangers we may find ourselves in. We can also recall how often delight and joy have come from unexpected, unpredicted events.

∽

Reflections on "Not Knowing"

Take a few minutes now to write about your thoughts and feelings on the fear of "not knowing." What are some situations in which you experience the fear of "not knowing"?

How do you sometimes react to that fear? What formulas have you tried to apply that no longer work for you?

Explore any subpersonalities you have that react to "not knowing." What are their catastrophic expectations? What are these subpersonalities forgetting about your inner resources? What do they need?

∽

Fearful subpersonalities may require focused attention to be calmed and strengthened. The exercises in chapter 6 may help; you can use your journal to write a dialogue with any such fearful subpersonality you have discovered.

Sometimes, however, it's possible to sense when we are partially identified in this way and simply choose to surrender to both the larger reality of who we really are and the interdependent web of life that sustains us. Then we don't have to "know" answers, solutions, or even what is going on. We can observe and trust the unfolding process from the abiding safety of Self.

When I am able to do this, when I can remember that there is more to reality than my current concepts and feelings, I feel enormous relief. After a few moments of free-fall and fear, as I let go of all the mental structures I have clung to for "safety," I discover I do not crash and burn. I feel the support of the universe. I find that life continues even without my conscious interventions. And the Mystery becomes wondrous rather than terrifying.

Out of its abysses, unpredictable life emerges, with a never-ending procession of miracles, crises, healing, and growth. Sometimes what happens is painful, tragic, seemingly unbearable to us mortals. Yet somehow life continues, also yielding an ample supply of beauty, pleasure, and fulfillment. When I realize this once again, I also see the absurdity of my belief that I can understand, predict, and control life. All I can really do is go along for the ride, with as much consciousness and love as I can muster in the moment.

OTHER DEMONS

Fear and anger are not our only demons. Some people suffer from chronic depression, from addictions or obsessions, from bitterness and cynicism, or from oppressively low self-esteem. Anger and fear may be at the root of some of these deeply ingrained conditions, but the exercises and thoughts shared here may not be enough to heal and transform them. This course is no substitute for psychotherapy; instead, I hope it may stimulate some readers to gather their courage and find a good therapist with whom they can continue exploring and growing.

Depression

Most of us struggle with these demons from time to time; most of us have felt discouraged, disillusioned, defeated, ashamed, bitter, and inadequate. Depression seems most common; if we don't feel discouraged and depressed occasionally in today's world, we are either enlightened spiritual masters or out of touch with the painful realities around us. Depression and related feelings may be signals that we need to grow and change. Such feelings may be healthy responses to problems that others are trying to pretend are not there. They may mean we are cutting off our life juices, living or working in conflict with our deepest values, dreams, and needs. In otherwise healthy people, short-term depression is as likely to come from a spiritual conflict as from a deficiency in one's personality or biochemistry.

We can work with depression in the same way we work with subpersonalities or with any strong feeling we discover in ourselves. Try the inner dialogue techniques described in chapter 6 and the awareness and centering techniques from chapters 1 and 3. Seek out the message behind the feelings: *What is my unconscious trying to say to me here? What energies or insights are wanting to emerge? Is my depression about my own personal life, or is it a response to pain around me or in the world? If I really let myself feel these feelings, what do I imagine would happen? Am I willing to take that risk and see what really does happen?*

Write your responses to these inquiries in your journal and see where the process goes. Record your feelings and thoughts as they move and change, noticing images and memories that arise. If you simply stay with your changing experience and follow it through to its completion, you may learn a great deal about yourself and come to a place of peace and resolution, at least for now. Recurring depression may need further exploration as you work through the layers of feelings, beliefs, and assumptions.

As we have discussed before, depression may also be a response to global threats. Joanna Macy has developed a profound healing process for people struggling, consciously and unconsciously, with this kind of despair.[2] This approach, also sometimes called "deep ecology," is extremely helpful in moving through and beyond our depression and despair about the state of the world. At the heart of the process is a group acknowledgement of the horror of what we face and the unexpressed feelings we carry in response. With group support and comfort, it is much easier to get in touch with these feelings. As the feelings are expressed in words and movement, they become less paralyzing, and people often find renewed commitment and determination to take positive action.

Shame

Another common demon is shame, which can poison our self-esteem and ability to develop our potential. Such "toxic" shame usually comes from childhood "shaming" and/or abuse and from parents crippled by alcoholism or their own abusive upbringings.[3] Most Western cultures have believed in shaming as a child-rearing technique for many generations, so most of us carry some shame into adulthood, even from relatively healthy families. Now we are beginning to see that shaming is nearly always destructive to self-esteem and self-confidence and should be replaced by more positive communication.

The next guided exercise offers a way of healing a childhood experience of shame. A similar process can be used for working through other traumatic childhood experiences.

∞

Healing Childhood Shame

Sitting in a comfortable, relaxed position, close your eyes and simply experience your breathing for several moments. Let your breathing carry your attention deep inside. Let your outside concerns fall away for now. . . .

When you are ready, recall a few times when you felt inappropriate shame, perhaps in a way that limited or constrained you. Let yourself relive the feelings of those experiences. . . .

Now go back to a time when you first remember feeling such feelings, a time in your early childhood. Let your imagination take you back, even if you can't recall a specific situation. . . .

Trust whatever images come, of a place and of yourself as a child in a scene. Notice who else is there, especially any adults, and what their relationships are to you. . . .

Now observe the scene from the outside, seeing yourself as the child while you remain as the adult you are now. Notice what is being said or done and how the child responds. Notice what the child feels. . . .

Speak now to the child you were, and let this child know you are present, and that you care for her or him. . . .

Let the child tell you how he or she feels. . . . What does the child really need?

Now imagine that you can step into the scene as a centered adult and intervene on the child's behalf. What would you say to the child? What would you say to the other people present? Tell them how to communicate their needs and concerns respectfully to the child, without making the child ashamed. . . .

If the other people in the scene are willing to try another way, replay the scene with them using the approach you have suggested. See how it works, how the child responds. . . .

If you want to make further changes in the interaction to better meet everyone's needs, do so. Replay the scene as often as necessary. . . .

When you have a sense of resolution, take some time with the child as she or he is now. How does the child feel about himself or herself?

Become the child and experience this from the inside. . . . Imagine growing up with this feeling of self-respect. . . .

Now remember the situations of shame you thought of at the beginning of this process. Choose one, and from a centered Observer perspective, send yourself in that situation a powerful beam of self-respect to replace any inappropriate shame you still feel. . . .

Then become yourself in the situation and imagine receiving that beam of self-respect. Really take it in. . . .

Write about the experience, referring back to the exercise instructions to remind yourself of the various steps.

∽

Shame Can Sometimes Be Appropriate

Shame is not always toxic. It is appropriate to feel some shame when we have done something that compromises our values, as we all do from time to time. We may also feel shame when we have not acted positively to intervene when witnessing someone else's unethical or immoral action. Fear, greed, or laziness may stop us from speaking or acting on another's behalf, and we feel ashamed that we have not lived up to our own ideals. This kind of shame generally has to do with actions actually hurtful to others rather than with merely unconventional social behavior. And we usually feel it spontaneously, on our own, not because someone else "shames" us.

Healthy shame reminds us of our deeper values and prods us into making amends. Such shame is rarely debilitating; it arises out of rather than undermines our self-respect and self-esteem. It actually helps us become more of who we really are. This is in marked contrast to "toxic shame," which makes us feel essentially bad about ourselves. Healthy shame is really a form of humility, the willingness to recognize one's limitations and to learn from one's mistakes.

SEEKING HELP WITH YOUR DEMONS

The demons of anger, fear, depression, shame, and others not specifically addressed here are common to us all. They seem to be a part of natural human response to life, and each is potentially valuable and potentially crippling. If any of these demons weighs heavily on your life, keeping you from wholeness, please seek help from a counselor or psychotherapist. Keep looking until you find one you trust, one who is caring and supportive of you and your deepest values. Then invest in your own well-being and the health of your family by working as long as you need to transform your demons into inner resources and strengths.

Addictions

If your demon takes the form of addiction to alcohol, other drugs, eating, sex, or abusive relationships, you may benefit from attending a support group for fellow sufferers. Alcoholics Anonymous is the best-known of these groups and has given rise to many others, such as Al-Anon, Alateen, Narcotics Anonymous, Adult Children of Alcoholics, Co-Dependents Anonymous, Overeaters Anonymous, and so on. These groups base their recovery work on the Twelve Steps and acknowledge the need for a spiritual awakening for true recovery.

Although many thousands have found the Twelve Step approach to be of help, it does not work for everyone. Other groups exist that use other approaches and models of recovery. Private counseling with a counselor knowledgeable about addictions is often helpful. Many of the exercises and ideas in this book will be helpful to readers already engaged in recovery programs.

Although the insights gained through the exercises in this chapter are a valuable step in the process of growing whole, we need more than insight. We must finally make choices about how we live our lives. In the next chapter, we will explore the "will." We will learn how to develop and use it gracefully in our daily lives for the benefit of ourselves, our families, and our world.

8. Living Will Fully

WE HAVE TAKEN THREE KEY STEPS in the process of psychosynthesis: we have clarified where we are now, what our emerging potential may be, and what might get in our way. We have a lot of information and insight, but is that enough? How often have you experienced an exciting "Eureka!" only to have it melt over time? Sometimes we do change spontaneously after moments of clarity and insight without being aware of having made any special choices. However, many moments of inspiration fail to materialize as positive change in life because they are not grounded in conscious choice and action.

What is needed, then, is the *will* to act upon our knowledge and insight. Our will is our power to choose, to bring about changes in ourselves, in others, and in our environment. It is the central force within us, intimately connected with Self. It is difficult to imagine discovering a deep sense of "Selfhood" without discovering the will, either first or simultaneously. To many people, the experience of having and being a will is their primary experience of Self.

A MATTER OF SURVIVAL

Today, perhaps more than ever before, we need to call upon our collective will for survival. And just as democracy depends on the participation of all its citizens, our collective will depends on the awakening and development of each of our personal wills. I cannot be empowered as a citizen if I am not first empowered as a person.

How have you experienced will in your life? Do you think of yourself as having a strong will? Take a few minutes to reflect on your past experiences of using your will to make easy and difficult decisions, to learn new skills, to overcome obstacles, to resolve interpersonal conflicts. What are some of the qualities of will you have experienced in your life? Is the will only a matter of determination, the stereotypical "stiff upper lip," or are there other dimensions to it? As we continue our discussion of the will, you may find your own experience of will reflected in some of the ideas offered.

WAYS OF WILLING

The will has a bad reputation with some folks. It is seen as a bludgeon with which to beat oneself up or a dogged stubbornness that pushes a person willy-nilly into action without regard for the feelings and interests of those around. A child who demands her own way is called "willful" and is said to need to be "taken down a peg." On the other hand, people are sometimes exhorted to exercise "willpower" to overcome undesirable habits, even addictions, as if all it took was a little more exertion.

Basically, these perspectives on the will are distortions of only one aspect of the will: strength. Certainly we need strength of will, but power alone is blind and insensitive: it can injure self and others, and can charge off in totally wrong directions. To be effective, our will needs two other dimensions: skillfulness and goodness. Willing is not simply bulldozing our way along; we can skillfully move over, under, and around obstacles in our path. We can also use feedback from the obstacles to change course altogether. And good will assures that our choices are in harmony with others and with our environment. Good will supplies the sensitivity we need.

Most of us can remember times in our lives when we acted on impulse, without skill or concern for harmony, with undesirable results. Or perhaps we forced ourselves to do something that turned out to be unhealthy for us in the long run, such as following a strict diet or staying in an unfulfilling job. Our will was active in these instances, but only in its "strong" dimension. It is experiences like these that give "will power" a bad name.

A Balance of Three Dimensions

Skillful will and good will can also be distorted, if they are not balanced by the other two dimensions. A person with skillful will without good will can be manipulative and deceptive. "Passive aggression"—undermining or striking out at others indirectly—is a classic example of very skillful will compensating for inadequate strength of will. Good will without skill or strength can create a lot of good intentions that never get carried out. A person of unbalanced good will may be crippled by guilt and low self-esteem.

How balanced is your will among these three dimensions? You can follow the suggestions on the next few pages to explore how your strong will, skillful will, and good will have been useful in your life in various situations. You may decide that you are well developed in one dimension, but need to work on another. The exercises that follow can help you develop all three.

◌

Strong, Skillful, and Good Will

What do you know about how you use each of these dimensions of will? Which seems most developed; which least developed? Write about a time you felt each one was particularly active in a situation or choice.

Which dimension of will do you most need to develop? Or do you need more integration of all three?

∞

DEVELOPING STRENGTH OF WILL

What do you associate with the term "strong will"? People with strong will are positively described as determined, courageous, decisive, and persistent. On the other hand, they may be called stubborn, headstrong, inflexible, and obstinate. If your associations are primarily in the latter group, you may need to revise your image of strong will to make it something more admirable and desirable to develop. Find the positive qualities of strong will that appeal to you, and imagine describing yourself in these terms. How would it be to think of yourself as decisive, courageous, tenacious? Would these attributes conflict with or support other valued images you hold of yourself?

Assagioli recommends several approaches to developing strength of will in both of his books, *Psychosynthesis* and *The Act of Will*. I have found the so-called useless exercises most helpful.

THE USELESS EXERCISE

The idea is to perform some simple, repetitive task for a fixed period of time, usually ten minutes, with no other purpose than to exercise the will. There should be no other payoff or reward, because that would involve "skillful will" and perhaps even "good will," while our purpose here is simply to experience and develop strength of will. Choose one of the following useless activities, or make one up, and decide before you begin how long you are going to perform the activity. Set a timer or have a clock in sight.

- Tie and untie your shoes.
- Put objects such as matches or toothpicks in a container and take them out again, repeatedly.
- Pick up a small object, such as a book. Carry it across the room, put it down, pick it up, and carry it back to its original place, repeatedly.
- Stand on a chair or in another designated spot doing nothing.

As you perform the task, notice what happens inside, what thoughts and feelings arise. Notice any rebellion or judgements and how you handle them. Keep on with your task until the time is up.

If you sense that this is a beneficial process for you, continue it for seven to ten days on a regular basis, keeping notes about your responses each day. Watch for changes, releases, and openings.

DEVELOPING SKILLFUL WILL

According to Assagioli, "The essential function of the skillful will . . . is the ability to develop that strategy which is most effective and which entails the greatest economy of effort, rather than the strategy that is most direct and obvious."[1] Using our will skillfully means expending less effort; that is a whole new angle on the will for many people. Strong will has

115

claimed so much attention that we may have overlooked the more subtle qualities of skillful will, such as attention and focus, patience and endurance, mastery and discipline, and organization, integration, and synthesis. Consider for a moment how many of these qualities apply to you, at least to some degree. You probably use the skillful aspect of your will more commonly in your daily life than you realize. Anytime you consider the consequences of an action and choose between alternatives, you are using skillful will. Anytime you try a new approach to an old problem, you are using skillful will. When a two-year-old starts to bang on your coffee table with a block and you distract her with another toy, you are using skillful will.

You have also used skillful will in many of the exercises you have done throughout this book, including the first writing exercise in this chapter. Whenever you look objectively at yourself and at your thoughts, feelings, needs, and desires, you are learning how to motivate yourself. That is what skillful will is all about. As Assagioli says, "The most effective and satisfactory role of the will is not as a source of direct power or force, but as that function which . . . can stimulate, regulate, and direct all the other functions and forces of our being so that they may lead us to our predetermined goal."[2] Obviously we need to be aware of all the "functions and forces of our being" if we are to "stimulate, regulate, and direct" them.

Assagioli's Star Diagram

Let's take a look at these functions and forces; they are not new to our study. Assagioli represented them in the "star diagram"[3] (see figure 2) as sensation, emotion, desire-impulse, imagination, thinking, and intuition. As you can see, the will is represented as the circle in the middle of the star, with "self" at its center. Thus self can coordinate all the functions and choose among them to fit the needs of the immediate situation. In the next exercise, which is adapted from work done by Louise McComber in Quebec, we'll touch on each of these functions within ourselves and see how we can develop and use them.

Figure 2 – Star Diagram

∽

Exploring the Star

Take a few moments to relax and pay attention to your breathing. Bring your attention within yourself, letting the outside world go for now. . . .

1.

Begin now to pay attention to the sensations in your body. Notice whatever claims your attention first. . . . Focus in on this sensation for a while. Does it give you any information?

Now notice the sensation of your body against the surface on which you are sitting. . . . Notice the temperature of the air around you. . . . Notice the relative tension in your shoulders and neck. . . .

When you direct your attention somewhere, you immediately become aware of sensations that were not in your field of awareness just before. Play with this ability for a few moments. . . .

Now look around you for a few moments. What do you see? What do you hear?

Close your eyes again, and move your arms around. How do you know where your arms are, and how they are moving? . . .

Have you ever been made to doubt your sensations, or to numb yourself against them? How did this affect your life? . . .

Take a few moments to appreciate the role of sensation in your life, something so basic that we take it for granted most of the time. . . . Then make some notes about sensation and its role in your life.

2.

Next, allow yourself to become aware of your desires and the energy of desiring. . . . How do you experience hunger? thirst? restlessness? sexual desire? How do you respond emotionally and mentally when you feel them?

Now recall a time when you were suddenly in physical danger and reacted out of instinct to save yourself. . . . Remember how it felt, and what the source of that impulse seemed to be. . . .

How have your desires and impulses been a problem for you? Have you ever been made to feel ashamed of them?

Affirm to yourself the value of your desires and impulses. How might you make better use of this dimension of your personality? Pause now to make notes if you want. . . .

3.

Now pay attention to your emotions. Begin by noticing any emotions you are feeling right now, perhaps in response to the exercise so far. . . .

Notice the obvious emotions you can name and the subtle ones that are harder to identify. . . . Remember feelings you had before starting to read just now, and notice whether they are still with you to some degree. . . .

Recall a time when you felt very angry, and notice if that feeling returns to you in part right now. . . . Recall other occasions when you felt happy . . . sad . . . excited . . . afraid. . . . Recall, if you can, a time when you seemed to feel no emotions at all; what was that like for you?

How have you been wounded emotionally in your life?

Affirm to yourself the valuable role your emotions play in your life. How might you use your emotions more consciously and harmoniously in your life? Pause now to make some notes. . . .

4.

When you are ready, give some attention to your thinking process. For a few moments, simply observe your thoughts going by . . . words, phrases . . . questions, associations, conclusions . . . ideas, insights, judgements . . . Notice how your mind moves here and there. . . .

What feelings come up as you observe your thoughts? What judgements do you have about your intelligence, your thinking ability? Have you experienced hurtful criticism about your thinking ability or style?

What role does thinking play in your life now? How is it important to you? How would you like to change or improve your thinking?

As with the other functions, affirm the specific value of thinking in your life . . . and pause to make some notes.

5.

Now let's pay attention to imagination. This function is a blend of thinking, feeling, and sensation. For a few moments, imagine yourself in a place you really would love to be. . . .

How did you do that? What senses did you use: vision, hearing, taste, smell, touch, movement? For a few minutes, play with your imagination, trying out all the different senses . . .

How has your imagination been supported or discouraged in your life? How has it caused you problems? How do you use it now for healing, creativity, and problem solving?

What would it be like to welcome imagination into your life even more? Are there specific areas in which you would like to do this?

Celebrate for a few moments the value of imagination to you, and then pause to make some notes. . . .

6.

Last but not least, we turn our attention to intuition. This important function was largely ignored by our civilization until recently, or at least mistrusted. Take a few moments to open your awareness to your intuitive faculties, your capacity to sense things beyond what you have learned or figured out with your thinking mind.

How do you experience your intuition? Through what other functions does it tend to come to you?

How do you distinguish intuition from desire and impulse, or from messages from various subpersonalities?

Do you ever feel the need to hide or disguise your intuition?

How do you use it for guidance and insight? Would you like to use intuition more in your life?

Affirm intuition as a full and valuable partner within your personality and make some notes about it. . . .

Now take a moment to hold all these functions in your awareness: sensation, desire/impulse, emotion, thinking, imagination, and intuition. All of these functions are available to you for skillful living, healing, creating, working, and playing. You are at the center; you are the center of awareness and will, which can harmonize and direct all these wonderful capacities in the unfolding of your life. . . .

Take plenty of time with this experience and in writing about any further thoughts, feelings, sensations, images, and so on.

∞

Choosing What to Develop

Consider for a moment a change you would like to make in your life, perhaps to overcome the blocks you explored in chapters 6 and 7. This change may be related to one or more of the six functions represented in the star diagram. If you want to develop courage, for example, that might relate to sensation, emotion, and imagination. Or you might find it relates more to your thinking or desire-impulse function. As we have noted many times, there are no formulas that apply uniformly to everyone.

No matter what changes you might want to make, you can bring any of these functions into play. To develop serenity, for example, you might practice sitting and moving in a serene fashion (sensation). You might notice when a desire tugs at you and use that as an occasion to invoke serenity. You might explore the emotions that commonly tend to upset your serenity and work with them as suggested in chapter 7. You might study serenity, its meaning and source, and read about people who are able to be serene in difficult circumstances (thinking). You might visualize yourself acting serenely in various upsetting situations (imagination). You might be able to sense the deeper unity within a conflict (intuition). Consider how you might use each of the six functions in making a desirable change in your life.

Two Techniques

Two "skillful will" techniques draw upon thinking, emotions, and sensation. One is the use of evocative words. Write the word for your quality on an index card. Write it in a style that fits the meaning of your word; for example, "courage" might be written in bold, block letters while "playfulness" might be written in a childish scrawl. Decorate your card appropriately, and then put it somewhere you will see it often, such as on the refrigerator door, on a mirror, or on the dashboard of your car. Every time you see the word, the quality is evoked in you, even without your conscious awareness.

The second technique is called "acting-as-if." Just as the name implies, you simply act as if you had your quality fully developed. You speak to others, and yourself, in terms that reflect this accomplishment. You make little choices from this perspective. You are practicing your new quality, trying it on for size, and in the process, you may discover it is already more developed within you than you believed.

A word of caution about acting-as-if: this technique should not be used to strengthen denial about one's contrary feelings or patterns. Acting courageous when one is terrified could mean suppressing the fearful feelings, which may find a destructive way of expressing themselves. It might lead to foolhardy behavior. Acting-as-if should always be done with full awareness of feelings and of the situation. On the stage, for example, the actor always remembers that he or she is performing.

DEVELOPING GOOD WILL

One of the reasons the will has such a bad reputation is the common notion that to be "willful" means to be selfish, to use one's will to further one's own "selfish" ends at the expense of others. And indeed, strong and skillful will can be used in this way, as Assagioli writes in *The Act of Will:*

> Selfishness springs from the desire to possess and to dominate, which is an expression of the basic urges of self-preservation and self-assertion. Inevitably it comes into collision with obstructions that block its satisfaction; aggressiveness and violence are thereby aroused, and the will [is] used to destroy whatever is interfering with the attainment of the desired objects. . . . The control of selfishness is . . . not only an ethical exigency; it is a necessity for the very safety of mankind. . . . The problem is mobilizing the will to good. . . .[4]

As we noted earlier, the will to good, or good will, assures that our choices are in harmony with others and with our environment. The principle of "enlightened self-interest" indicates that such choices will almost always be to our best advantage too. Good will is not enough, however, because without skill or strength, we may create a lot of good intentions that never get carried out. And if we become overly concerned with meeting the needs and desires of others, we may be crippled by guilt and low self-esteem. So how do we develop a balanced, healthy good will?

Good will is one of those archetypes so basic to our values that it is difficult to define. What is your sense of it? When you read or hear that someone is "a person of goodwill," what do those words mean to you? When you feel "good will" toward someone, how do you experience that?

Take a few minutes to write about good will, its meaning to you, its importance in your life. Recall when it has been a strong force in you, and when it has not. What enables you to have good will, to act from good will? If you have a well-developed good will, but not enough skillful or strong will, how has that caused you difficulties?

◇

Guided Receptive Meditation on Good Will

Sitting comfortably, relax your body, and breathe easily, with awareness. Imagine sinking into yourself to a place of peace and clarity. Take time. . . .

For a few minutes, review in your mind the thoughts, feelings, ideas, and experiences of good will you have just written down. Imagine gathering them all together in an open container such as a basket or a bowl. Add any new thoughts, feelings, or imaginings about good will that come to you now. . . . Imagine holding all this knowledge gently, loosely, in this container before you. . . .

Now allow an image to come, an image that represents "good will" to you. The image may come through any of your inner senses. Trust whatever comes. Wait patiently for it to become clear to you. . . .

Imagine putting your image of good will into your container too, along with any additional insights or feelings. . . .

Now hold your container up to the sun, allowing the warm light to fall upon it all. Ask for more wisdom to come to you, to illuminate your relationship to good will and whatever problems you may have with good will in your life. . . .

Wait patiently for whatever will come. You may receive more images or insights right away, or sometime later. Just allow your experience, whatever it may be. . . .

Now look into your container again, to see what changes, if any, have occurred. Take in whatever wisdom you find there. . . . When you are ready, draw your image and write about your experience in your journal.

∽

Ultimately Spiritual

As you may have discovered, good will is ultimately spiritual. Because it has to do with our relationship to those around us, it demands a sense of connection, empathy, even love, and these are all spiritual values. It is more difficult, therefore, to prescribe a technique for developing good will; the impulse has to come from deep within us. Developing good will may depend on overcoming some of the blocks we addressed in the previous two chapters, because fear, anger, and old wounds may inhibit our good will. They may convince us that we had better watch out for Old Number One as opposed to the welfare of those around us. We may first need to develop good will toward ourselves before we can offer it to others.

Balancing Love and Will

Good will has a lot to do with love, in the highest sense of the word. Often, in our society at least, love and will seem to be in opposition. Certainly most national foreign policy reflects this; we seem far more concerned with imposing our national will upon other nations than we are with building loving relationships with them. Or to put it more precisely, governmental leaders are often more concerned with imposing their will upon the leaders of other nations—and upon their own people—than they are about building loving relationships between nations.

Perhaps this is because we fear that if we get too loving, we will lose our will; we will become weak, ineffectual, easy to exploit and overthrow. But weakness does not come from love, but rather from a failure of will. When we are afraid of losing someone else's love and approval, we may give up our power and responsibility to choose right action and stand our ground. In this case, we are not acting out of love at all, but out of fear.

Part of our problem with "love" is our confusion about romantic love, which—at least as portrayed in the media—is a kind of addiction. This kind of romantic love seems to demand all kinds of compromises of one's personal welfare. It may take the form of a man demanding that his wife give up her career to accommodate his, or a woman demanding constant verbal interaction from her introverted husband. If we tried to satisfy the criteria for "loving" from this point of view, we would indeed be weak, ineffectual, and open to exploitation.

I believe even true romantic love is compatible with a strong, skillful, and good will. A supportive, nurturing relationship between any two people, whether business partners, friends, relatives, or lovers, is built on a foundation of wholeness within each individual. In this kind of relationship, to act out of love means to choose action of benefit to both self and other, at the deepest level, even if the other makes demands to the contrary.

We really can have both love and will in balance; most of our personal, social, and international problems would benefit from such a balance. We need both love and will, sensitivity and determination, acceptance and choice. Love, and the balance of love and will, are explored further in chapter 11, "Relationships: Growing Whole Together."

TRANSPERSONAL WILL

We go along making decisions and choices, sometimes with awareness, sometimes hardly thinking about them. Most of our choices have to do with personal survival and welfare, with family and work concerns, with maintaining a pleasant living environment, and with meeting various personal needs and desires. We experience our personal will, strong, skillful, and even good, in making these decisions and choices. And sometimes something beyond this occurs. We feel a "call" or inner prompting to act beyond our own immediate welfare and gratification. Our personal will is drawn into alignment with a "Higher Will" and we choose a whole new direction, or act purely for the benefit of others, even at the expense of some personal comfort.

Many of us can recall making a decision beyond our "comfort zone"—to go back to school; to change careers or jobs; to take on a difficult task; to begin to draw or paint, dance, or play a musical instrument; to help some person or group in need; or to commit our energies to a cause. Such decisions may be accompanied by a lot of inner turmoil and doubt; they may require considerable adjustment in our lifestyle and routine. Yet something in us demands that we take that course, no matter what. That "something" may be Transpersonal Will, the Will of Self.

In the following exercise, you can explore one or more of these decisions, and clarify for yourself what "Transpersonal Will" is in your own experience. And it is very important to rely on your own experience about such concepts as Self and Transpersonal Will, instead of using someone else's definitions. Definitions and descriptions, when set down authoritatively, tend to become dogmatic and exclude any unusual experiences that depart from a crystallized "truth." Let's avoid that, if possible.

∽

An Experience of Transpersonal Will

Sitting comfortably, relax your body, and breathe easily, with awareness. Imagine sinking into yourself, to a place of peace and clarity. Take time to come to center. . . .

Now recall a time when you made an important life decision that you believe now to have been a good one, even though at the time you may have had some doubts. Recall the decision, and the circumstances surrounding it. You may recall more than one; if so, choose one to work with now.

Now review the events, inner and outer, that led up to your decision. When did you first start considering this choice, and what prompted you to consider it? Did the idea come to you suddenly, or recurrently over time?

How did you react to this idea? Did you feel some resistance? Where did the resistance come from, and what form did it take? How did you deal with it?

What strengthened your resolve to make this decision? What rational arguments did you muster? What role did your emotions play? What role did your intuition play?

Did you seek help and advice from others? What methods did you use to help you clarify your thoughts and feelings (such as meditation, prayer, counseling, or journaling)?

Can you recall how and when the decision was actually made? How did you feel and act then?

What were the repercussions in your life, inside and out, and how did you handle them? What enabled you to carry through with your decision?

Take some time to remember anything else about this experience that you think is important. Try to find the essence of this experience in your body, feelings, and mind. Take all the time you need, and when you are ready, make some notes in your journal.

∞

Mysterious Ways

Transpersonal Will works in our lives in mysterious ways; it may prompt us to move in directions that don't "make sense" to our current understanding of ourselves and the world. Yet it does operate according to natural law, at least in my experience. It is just that we don't know everything about how life works! If we maintain humility about our knowledge and comprehension of life, we are always open to new possibilities and new adventures.

In chapter 10, "What to Do When We See the Light," we will further explore transpersonal experiences, including those of Transpersonal Will. For now, you may want to explore other life decisions using the preceding exercise to discover how they may have been guided by the Will of your Self.

In the next chapter, you will be able to put the principles of "living will fully" into practice in making choices for your life right now. Every time we act consciously, using our will in all its dimensions, we experience Self, the center of our Being, in harmony with the larger Whole of life.

9. Choosing to Change

WE HAVE ALL MADE MANY CHOICES IN OUR LIVES, and some of them have actually "worked." We have changed a habit, made a move, developed a skill, or learned a better way of interacting. Not all our choices pan out that well, however; think of all the New Year's resolutions that have fallen by the wayside, sometimes by January 2! Or sometimes we may have continued stubbornly on a chosen path long after it was clear, at least to those around us, that it was not in our best interest.

What makes a choice "work"? And how do we know we are making the "right" choice at any given time? What about when we make a wrong one?

DECISIONS NEED BROAD PERSPECTIVES

Many choices are made in haste, without our using our skillful or good will adequately, or without sufficient evoking of our strong will. We may think we want a particular change but fail to consult the parts of ourselves that have other ideas. Contrary motivations may subvert the best of intentions. We may define our goal too narrowly, without sufficient flexibility to respond to the vicissitudes of external events. Or we may base a choice on insufficient information with little thought about alternatives, and live to regret it.

In previous chapters, we have explored a series of three questions through imagery and drawing. In chapter 2, we asked, "Where am I now in my life?" In chapter 5, "What is emerging for me now in my life?" In chapter 6, "What is getting in my way?" These questions enable us to step back, look at the big picture of our lives, and see where we want to go in a general, holistic way. Choices made from this perspective will more likely be meaningful, significant, and in our overall best interest. They are more likely to take into account all the various parts of ourselves and all the contrary motivations. And because the perspective is broad, our choices will be less dependent on external events being a certain way.

The following exercise may help you determine a course of action or direction that will move you toward your potential (second question) and transform your blocks (third question). It asks the question, "What do I need to develop?" Some of the responses people have to this question suggest qualities such as strength, love, determination, or faith. Your response will be unique to your situation and potential, and may be unexpected. Trust whatever images come in response to the question, and wait until you are finished before trying to figure out what they mean.

Before beginning, review your drawings and notes on the first three questions. If a lot has changed since you did these drawings, it might be a good idea to redo the whole series in preparation for this final step.

∞

What Do I Need to Develop?

Take a few moments to relax and bring your attention within yourself, letting the outside world go for now. Breathe. . . .

Move to the place within where you find answers to your deepest questions, where you can ask and wait for an inner response. . . .

Now ask yourself, *What do I need to develop in order to move through the blocks toward my potential? What quality do I need the most at this time in my life?*

Notice any images, visual or kinesthetic, that come to mind. Notice sounds, feelings, impressions of all kinds. . . . What do I need to develop in my life now?

When you feel ready, record your inner responses and images in a drawing. . . . Make some notes on your feelings and thoughts about the drawing. . . .

Now close your eyes again and return to a relaxed, inward state. Allow your breathing to become easy and full. . . .

Think of a situation in your daily life in which this quality would be especially useful, where it would help you move toward your potential more fully. You might think of a situation at work, with your family, with friends, or alone. . . .

Now imagine yourself full of this quality and acting from it. See what effect this has on the situation. Notice how you feel. . . .

Do this with a couple of other situations if you wish. . . .

Stand up for a moment, keeping your focus inward, and experience this quality within your body. Try moving as if this quality were already developed within you. . . .

When you feel complete, brainstorm for some ideas about how to develop this quality more in your life. Don't censor yourself; write down any ideas, no matter how absurd they might seem at the moment. Include all the various aspects of your life in your brainstorming.

Now that you have a sense of a quality or set of qualities you need to develop, you have the makings of a Will Project through which you can explore and develop your will. In fact, you have already begun your Will Project by visualizing your quality in various situations and by brainstorming ways to develop it further.

Of course, you are not limited to this particular theme. Your work with subpersonalities and inner demons or concerns in your daily life may suggest another change you want to make. You might want to quit smoking, make an important decision, improve your relationship with a family member or friend, or become more effective as an activist.

For the Will Project, we'll use the six stages that Assagioli describes in *The Act of Will*.[1] They are as follows:

1. Purpose
2. Deliberation
3. Choice
4. Affirmation
5. Plan
6. Implementation and evaluation

It is not necessary to go through each stage consciously, step-by-step, every time you make a choice. But to do so now will help reveal the value of each step and perhaps clarify where some of your past choices have gone astray.

STAGE ONE
CLARIFYING PURPOSE

Any meaningful activity in which we engage has a purpose, an underlying motivating force that can pour forth in myriad strategies and forms. When purpose is clear, our strong and skillful will can be brought to bear; we can be quite creative in accomplishing that purpose. Without a clear sense of purpose, however, we often become caught up in the form itself, the specific action, mistaking the means for the ends. We forget why we are doing something and our actions become mechanical and hackneyed.

A person with anorexia, for example, is obsessed with strict diet and exhaustive exercise long past the point of feeling and being healthy. A doctor who forgets that her purpose is helping her patients to heal may, out of habit, prescribe a treatment that is actually detrimental to a particular patient. When I lose touch with my purpose in writing this book—to share the principles and techniques of psychosynthesis to help transform our way of living—my writing dries up and I find myself grinding out stilted paragraphs without any joy. Recalling and redefining purpose in any activity can enliven and sustain us, even in times of stagnation or adversity. Remembering what it is all about makes the rough times more tolerable.

Make a Statement of Purpose

Your response to the last exercise may be formulated into a statement of purpose. If you discovered, for example, that what you need to develop is faith, then your purpose might simply be that: to develop faith. Or you might want to elaborate on the concept and state it something like this: "My purpose is to surrender each moment to faith in my own inner voice." Take time to find your own best wording for your purpose. You may find it nearly impossible to capture your sense of purpose in words, but it is helpful to try; for the very process of struggling for words will help you clarify what your purpose really is.

People sometimes describe their deep purpose with statements like these: "My purpose is to express love." "My purpose is to allow Spirit to flow through me." "My purpose is to experience connectedness to all there is." These statements might sound almost corny out of context, but they express meaningful experiences and basic values. It doesn't matter how your statement of purpose might sound to anyone else; if it speaks to a significant experience within you, it will infuse your actions and choices in a very positive way.

Take a few minutes now to formulate a statement of purpose for your Will Project.

An exercise for exploring purpose was offered in chapter 5 (see pages 68-69). It would be useful to review that exercise now and even repeat it. Through that process, you may have discovered a very profound, even spiritual, sense of purpose.

How is that sense of purpose related to the quality you need to develop? How is it related to the statement of purpose you just composed? Can the two be combined in a meaningful way?

Your sense of purpose may seem too abstract to be very useful or practical, and you may need to "step it down" to a more specific, everyday kind of statement for it to guide your practical choices. Do not forget, however, the larger purpose that encompasses the concrete goal. My immediate purpose, or goal, may be to develop a daily exercise routine, but I need to constantly remind myself that my larger purpose is to live fully and deeply each moment. Then my choices will be infused with this positive energy, instead of being focused on self-judgement about whether or not I follow my routine precisely. I might even choose to depart from my routine on occasion in order to enjoy some other enlivening activity that furthers my larger purpose.

You have clarified your purpose, at least to some extent. Now you are ready to go on to the next step.

Once we have a purpose in mind, we need to decide how to go about accomplishing it. We usually have many paths available to us, especially if we take the time to think about it. That is what the stage of deliberation is about: finding and considering alternative courses of action, assessing resources and barriers, and evaluating consequences. This is where skillful will really comes into play, finding the course of action that is most efficient and effective and which takes into account both external and internal conditions.

Brainstorming, meditation, inspiration and intuition, logical thought, reading, counseling, and consulting with others all can contribute to deliberation. With your purpose in mind, let's try out each of these possibilities.

Brainstorming means thinking up all kinds of possibilities, temporarily suspending judgement and evaluation. The idea is to turn our creativity loose so that ideas come to mind that might be ignored if we were being "sensible." A crazy idea can open up new areas for consideration, even though the specific idea may not seem practical. Brainstorming is usually done in groups, with someone recording all the suggestions as they come, often fast and furiously. You can brainstorm by yourself, however, letting the group of your subpersonalities all throw in their two cents worth.

You might take a few minutes now to do this. Write your purpose statement (the more concrete one) and then, beneath it, note everything that comes to mind as a way you could move toward, or accomplish, that purpose. Include both crazy and sensible ideas. Also include various aspects of your life: personal, familial, professional, social, and spiritual.

Tools That May Be Helpful

Meditation, inspiration, and intuition are closely related processes. One method of receiving inspiration is the Wise Person meditation, which appears in chapter 4. Use the process now to consult with your Wise Person about your purpose and the best way you might move in that direction.

Ask your Wise Person about some of the ideas you found through brainstorming. The Wise Person may also suggest some other avenues you have not yet considered.

Writing a letter to Self may also bring intuition and inspiration to bear in your deliberations. That process is described in chapter 3.

Meditating on the quality you need or on your statement of purpose will help you see your path more clearly; I recommend you include these concerns in whatever meditation you now practice, if you do. (We will explore Assagioli's recommended approach to meditation in chapter 10; because of the practice time required, however, we will not focus on it now.)

At this point, you probably have several good ideas to choose from in pursuing your purpose. It may be time to apply some logical thought. Choose three of those good ideas, and taking each in turn, think and maybe write about its pros and cons, the resources you have available to assist you in that area, possible roadblocks and how you might deal with them, and the various consequences, positive and negative, that might ensue. Notice how you feel as you do this.

Ways of Exploring and Evaluating Possibilities

Consulting with others and reading are obvious ways of exploring and evaluating possibilities. I personally find it a real challenge to keep my mind both open and discriminating while doing so. I want to hear others' ideas and perspectives, but I need to sort through them to find what is of value to my situation and what is aligned with my needs and purposes. No one is a better authority about what is right for me than I am, but I learn so much from others and am often inspired by another's vision, wisdom, and example.

Talking with a friend or counselor can often help us clarify our own ideas and motivations, sort out our fears and limiting beliefs, and reassure us that our decisions make sense. The process itself may actually be of greater value than any specific advice we receive from others. So we need to choose people who can really listen, who can empathize with our struggles, and who can share our vision of purpose. And we need to be patient with our friends' mistakes. As listeners we all get caught in wanting to help, or we forget to listen in our eagerness to tell our own stories of success and failure. Consider some people you might talk to about your purpose and potential choices, and some books or other media you might consult for more information and ideas.

At some point, we have to bring our deliberations to a close and make a choice. There is probably always more that we can consider in making a choice, and we can never be sure that we have explored everything possible. Yet we must choose, for to delay choice is itself a choice that has consequences in our lives. It is wonderfully freeing to realize, however, that nothing is set in concrete. We can always reconsider, deliberate, and choose again.

STAGE THREE
CHOICE

What do you choose to do to carry out your purpose? It

may be very clear to you after deliberating; you may even have several actions you wish to take. Or you may still feel uncertain about which way to go. The act of choosing can give us useful information. It is also very empowering. So let's proceed and see what happens.

◌

Exercise: To Choose or Not to Choose

Recall your statement of purpose. If it has changed in the course of your deliberation, consider it in its new formulation.

Now think of one action you are considering that you believe will further your purpose. (Examples: "Write in my journal every morning." "Spend more time with my kids.")

Complete each of the statements below with your action. (For example, after "I want to . . . ," you would say "I want to write in my journal every morning.") Say each statement aloud and notice about how it feels.

I want to . . .
I'll try to . . .
I wish I could . . .
I hope to . . .
I should . . .
I could . . .
I intend to . . .
I will . . .
I choose to . . .

Notice which statement seems most positive and strong to you. Say it to yourself several times, using different inflections and voice tones.

◌

Avoiding Choice

You may realize that one or more of the weaker statements in the exercise is quite familiar to you. Most of us use these statements to avoid making a choice. By saying these things to ourselves, and to others, we think we can demonstrate our good intentions while we leave the door open to changing our minds and to the barriers the circumstances of life may present. Remember the old saying, "The road to hell is paved with good intentions." We know from our study of the will in the previous chapter that although good will is very important, it needs strong and skillful will to be complete. For most of us, the early statements on the list lack these aspects.

If one of the statements toward the end of the list, or one you've composed, feels strong and good for you, then you have made your choice. This stage is nothing more than that: making a clear choice and knowing you have done so. If the last two or three statements felt uncomfortable, however, you may need to reconsider your options. Is your action too big a step? Are you taking into account all the obstacles in your way? Could you use skillful will to find a way through those obstacles?

This might be a good time to make some notes about your choice and your feelings about it now. Write it again in the strongest form.

STAGE FOUR
AFFIRMATION

Choice and affirmation are close to the same thing. When we make a strong, conscious choice and state it to ourselves, we are affirming that choice. Affirmation is skillful will in action, energetically gathering our emotions, imagination, sensations, desires, and thoughts behind our choice.

It is so important to feel good about our choices! We need to take the time to experience the strength and joy that consciously choosing can bring. We need to "psyche ourselves up" for what may be the hard work of carrying out our choices. And at the heart of it all, we each need to experience ourselves as "One Who Chooses." This is what affirmation is all about.

Verbal affirmations should also be stated in the most positive terms possible and in the present tense. For example, if your choice is to avoid driving faster than the speed limit, it would be more affirming to state it positively: "I drive comfortably at legal speeds." This statement means that your choice is happening now; it is not just a goal for the future.

You have already affirmed your choice, by writing it in a clear way, by finding the strongest phrasing for your statement of choice. You have affirmed it by saying it out loud to yourself. Now write a "formal" present-tense, positive affirmation of your choice.

Tell Someone About Your Choice

You can carry your affirmation further by telling someone close to you about your choice. See how it sounds to this other person. Ask for support. This is the step of "going public" with a choice, which often makes us feel more committed and certain about it.

On the other hand, it may be more affirming to you to decide to keep it private. If you are a more extroverted person who tends to share your plans with others, it may make your choice more special and significant to keep it secret, between you and your Self. Every time you feel tempted to tell someone about it but decide to keep it secret again, you are affirming your choice as well.

Make up a "mantra" for yourself, a short, meaningful phrase you can say over and over like a chant to yourself. Sing about it, either using a familiar song that reminds you of your choice or composing a new song for the occasion.

Write your choice on a card, or use just a few key words, and decorate it appropriately. Place this card where you will see it often, such as on a mirror, the refrigerator door, or the dashboard of your car. This is the "evocative word card" technique described in chapter 8.

Practice postures and movements that reflect your choice. Experience your affirmation in your body through dance.

One of the most powerful techniques of affirmation is visualization. Try this out in the following exercise.

∞

Imagery for Affirmation

Take a few moments to center and quiet your body, feelings, and mind. Breathe and notice. . . .

Picture yourself carrying out your choice in a realistic life situation. Imagine doing this with ease and enthusiasm. Imagine others responding positively, or at least neutrally. It may help to close your eyes to do this. . . .

If you imagine encountering difficulties, affirm your choice again to yourself and send that positive energy to yourself in your imagery. Picture yourself being strengthened by that energy and acting with ease to carry out your choice. . . .

Now step into your imagery and feel what it is like to be carrying out this choice. Feel the strength and mastery in your body, feelings, and mind. . . .

Visualize others around you responding positively to your chosen behavior. See and feel the beneficial effects of your choice. . . .

Repeat this visualization process several times a day, until it becomes natural to you. Make some notes about this process in your journal.

∞

Effective Visualization Follows Deliberation

All forms of affirmation, and especially visualization, are most effective when they follow the kind of deliberation we did in Stage Two. Then we can be more certain that our choice is indeed appropriate, harmonious, and realistic. If we leap from desire to visualization without clarifying our purpose and without adequate deliberation, we may waste a lot of time fantasizing about the impossible, yearning for things we don't really want or need.

Visualization may give us more information about the appropriateness of our choice; it might even prompt us to reconsider it altogether. This is, after all, a circular process that can return to earlier stages whenever it may be useful. On the other hand, some of the resistances we encounter at this point may simply be old habits that can be noted and set gently aside.

Take some time now to make sure you have affirmed your choice and feel ready to move into the planning and implementation of that choice. If your choice has changed somewhat, reaffirm it now.

STAGE FIVE
PLANNING

This stage is related to the earlier deliberation stage, often drawing upon ideas and information generated there. Taking into account various obstacles and concerns, how shall we proceed with our choice? Are there arrangements to be made, people to consult, a timetable to be set? It might be helpful to set up some contingency plans if our course of action may be affected by outside events or forces.

Planning is an activity most of us are fairly comfortable doing; it is more in the mainstream of our conscious lives. Our challenge here is to draw upon our skills in planning without losing sight of our purpose and our larger context for our choice and our actions. Our plans must be practical and concrete, but they also need to remain flexible and open to new inspiration.

∞

Reflections on Planning

Take a few minutes to consider how you usually plan. Is it a logical, conscious process for you, or more intuitive and implicit? Do you write things down, or just think about them informally? Are you able to change plans easily? On the other hand, are you able to stick to a plan when you encounter difficulties? . . .

Now, think about how you will carry out the choice you have just made and affirmed. Consider the steps you need to take, as you foresee them now, and make an estimate of when you can carry them out. . . .

What other people, if any, need to be involved? How will you communicate with them? What problems do you anticipate? How will you deal with these problems? . . .

Close your eyes and visualize yourself carrying out your plan and dealing with the problems. . . . Make notes about what you imagine happening and any changes you want to make in your plans.

∞

Planning is often combined with the next stage of implementation. We make some plans, try them out, and then decide what to do next. It seems rather obvious, doesn't it? Yet somehow we do get into trouble in this stage. We go off half-cocked and find ourselves in situations for which we are not prepared. Or we plan down to the smallest detail, become attached to our plan, and cannot change when circumstances demand it. Or we may succeed in carrying out our plan, but without the joy of spontaneity or of learning something new.

Take a look at your plan and see how it feels to you. Is it attractive to you? Is there room for play and spontaneous creativity? Are you willing to change it if it doesn't seem to work?

STAGE SIX
IMPLEMENTATION AND EVALUATION

Finally, it's time to act, to put our choice into motion. It's also time to stay alert, observe, and see what happens. Stay loose, flexible, open to change. We embark on the implementation of our Will Projects with curiosity and wonder. It is only an experiment, after all. We will try out this choice, this plan, and find out a little more about ourselves, about life, about the world around us.

We call upon all three aspects of will as we implement our choice. We use strong will to persevere when we encounter difficulties. We use skillful will to respond to changing circumstances, inside and out. We use good will to assure that our actions are harmonious with those around us and our environment.

We also call upon all our psychological functions: sensation, desire-impulse, emotion, thinking, imagination, intuition. We continually make little choices about how and when we call these various functions into play. Increasingly, we rely on our unconscious to carry forth our choice; through all the preparatory stages, we have been essentially tuning our unconscious for this end. And we stay aware, noticing inner responses and outward effects.

As you carry out your choice, keep notes in your journal of what occurs. If you need several days or weeks to implement it, write about its unfolding every day or so. Remember that this Will Project is an opportunity to explore in-depth the process of choosing to change.

Let It All Go

Then let it all go and carry on with life. We can become too obsessed with Making Conscious Choices, failing to trust ourselves and our unconscious. This six-stage model of an act of will is only a model, useful for deepening our understanding of this basic life process, but not intended to be a rigidly prescribed procedure for all occasions. Once we have gone through the process, the model will remain a useful set of guidelines that we can consult when needed for difficult choices and major decisions.

PURPOSE AND THE PLANET

Let's take a look now at how these stages of an act of will might be used collectively for the good of the planet. What if we applied this process to every project with a potential impact on others and the environment? Simply clarifying purpose would have a profound effect! And if choices were made on the basis of this deeper purpose, they would be far more likely to be aligned with the welfare of the community and environment.

Many times social activists get so caught up in their cause that they forget their underlying purposes. They may fail to give sufficient time to deliberation and go off half-cocked. They may undermine their effectiveness in the community through poor planning. They may burn out because they don't gather support for their decisions through affirmation. I urge you to try using these stages explicitly in any social or political action you undertake with others.

Through these first nine chapters, we have laid a foundation of principles and skills for conscious living. I hope the ideas and exercises offered here have enabled you to discover a deeper, stronger sense of Self, to explore and integrate the various dimensions of your personality, and to experience the power of the conscious use of will. The following three chapters apply these basic principles and skills to the challenges of spiritual awakening, relationship, and service. Read on!

10. What to Do When We See the Light

Who shall ascend into the hill of the Lord? Or who shall stand in His holy place? There is no one but us. There is no one to send, not a clean hand, nor a pure heart on the face of the earth, nor in the earth, but only us, a generation comforting ourselves with the notion that we have come at an awkward time, that our innocent fathers are all dead—as if innocence had ever been—and our children busy and troubled, and we ourselves unfit, not yet ready, having each of us chosen wrongly, made a false start, failed, yielded to impulse and the tangled comforts of pleasures, and grown exhausted, unable to seek the thread, weak, and involved. But there is no one but us. There never has been.[1]

—Annie Dillard

GROWING WHOLE is a spiritual endeavor. When we expand our awareness, strengthen our center, clarify our purpose, transform our inner demons, develop our will, and make conscious choices, we are moving toward deeper connection with our spiritual Self, or Spirit—however we name it. Wholeness and spirituality are intertwined.

Every now and then, however, life takes us in a big leap forward, sometimes, it seems, by the scruff of our necks. Mysterious forces, inside and out, demand changes in priorities, activities, relationships, and life directions. We are confronted with deeper issues of life and death, meaning and

149

purpose. These are times of "spiritual awakening" or "spiritual emergence."

WE MAY BE FACING A CRITICAL TIME

Many believe that we are all facing such a time now, the whole human race. The destructive effects of the modern industrial machine on the ecosystem of the planet, coupled with the horrendous power of our weapons technology, have brought us collectively to a crisis of survival. And this crisis of survival can be resolved only through a spiritual transformation. In truth, had we not suffered from increasing spiritual impoverishment during the twentieth century, we might have seen the error in our ways much sooner.

In a recent sermon at the Unitarian Universalist Fellowship of Sonoma County, the minister, Dan O'Neal, spoke to this spiritual impoverishment when he said that Western culture today has a "profoundly secular stance." Our whole culture lacks "a sense of being embedded in, and participants of, a larger sacred immensity. The way we are living on the planet is profoundly profane."[2] Vaclav Havel, who was the first democratically elected president of Czechoslovakia, speaks to the same concern in a recent essay:

> It may seem like a paradox, but one I think will prove true, that only through directing ourselves toward the moral and the spiritual can we arrive at a state in which life on this earth is no longer threatened by some sort of "megasuicide" and has a genuinely human dimension. This spiritual renewal is not something that one day will drop out of heaven into our laps, or be ushered in by a new Messiah. It is a task that confronts us all, every moment of our existence. We all can and must do something about it; we can't wait for anyone else.[3]

A SPIRITUAL AWAKENING AND RENEWAL

Havel echoes the theme of the Annie Dillard quotation introducing this chapter: we are all we've got to work with. There is no one else. If we are to survive as a species on this planet, you and I, and many others just like us, must separately and together find our way to spiritual awakening and renewal.

As we as individuals experience spiritual awakening, we learn how to awaken ourselves as a species. However, individual awakening cannot be that of the individualist seeking personal "salvation" and spiritual bliss in isolation from the world around us. Our awakening must be akin to that of the Bodhisattvas in the Buddhist tradition, who, on the threshold of Nirvana, turn back to the world because they realize they cannot be truly free until all beings are free.

Many Forms

Spiritual awakening takes many forms that are often unique to the individual. It may come as a strange sense of disorientation as familiar patterns of activity inexplicably lose their appeal. Life events may call our priorities and values into question. Awakening may come in the form of an artistic urge, a strong impulse to express one's self in color, shapes, textures, music, or dance. It may come as an overwhelming experience of despair at the suffering and destruction in the world. It may come as a vision to create something of service to the world, such as an organization, an instrument or tool, or a new model for understanding a facet of our universe.

Religious experiences of all kinds may be spiritual awakenings, including mystical moments when we "see the Light." So may be paranormal phenomena such as "out-of-body" experiences, clairvoyance, mental telepathy, or receiving messages that apparently come from other beings. It may come to us through the illness or death of a loved one or from suffering a debilitating or life-threatening illness ourselves.

Spiritual awakening may begin in experiences in the waking state, or it may first nudge us in dreams. It may even express itself through unexpected behavior when we find ourselves acting with unusual effectiveness, without conscious, logical thought. We may take whole courses of action and make major life decisions without fully realizing their significance until later. It just feels right. Many people speak of "being guided" by a wisdom beyond their rational mind.

Sometimes we may not recognize what is happening; we may think we are losing our grip, going nuts, or, more prosaically, experiencing "burnout." In time, however, we realize that we are faced with a challenge of a decidedly spiritual flavor. A new set of clothes or a few days off work isn't going to make everything "normal" again. Something radically different is required.

How to Know If It's a Real Awakening

Unfortunately, some of the experiences mentioned above could be signs of psychological breakdown rather than spiritual awakening. How do we distinguish between awakening and pathology? One criterion is the quality of the experience. For example, I might have an experience of "hearing voices" from within. If, on the one hand, the inner "voices" tell me to hurt myself or another, I need to seek professional psychological help.

If, on the other hand, my inner "voices" are loving, wise, and constructive in their advice, and if I can remain fairly centered and objective in listening to them, the experience may help me tap into the wisdom of my own superconscious. A therapist with a spiritual orientation, a pastor, or experienced spiritual guide can help sort this out.

Consider for a few minutes experiences you have had that might have been spiritual awakenings. Some you may have recognized at the time; others you may have ignored and suppressed. Were they artistic, creative, social, scientific, religious, healing, or paranormal in nature? What were your reactions to these experiences?

How can we best respond? We can start by practicing all the centering methods described in chapter 3. We can write and draw in our journals. We can seek the help of a pastor or spiritual counselor, or a therapist with a spiritual/transpersonal orientation. We can meditate, pray, study spiritual teachings, and spend quiet time in nature. We need to allow the awakening process to unfold in its own way as we observe and cooperate with it as best we can.

Most meditation techniques emphasize the breath. Thich Nhat Hanh, a Vietnamese Buddhist teacher and peace activist, suggests following the breath in this way: as you breathe in, say to yourself, "breathing in," and as you breathe out, say, "breathing out."[4] Do this simple practice with a sense of wonder at the miracle of breathing.

After a little practice with this, begin to include other experiences: "Breathing in, I feel tension in my shoulders. Breathing out, I release that tension." Or, "Breathing in, I feel afraid. Breathing out, I feel afraid." The experience being "breathed" may change or may continue for a while. The purpose is simply to notice what you experience and breathe with it all. This is especially useful in times of stress, strong feelings, and unnerving events. It provides a moment's pause to recollect yourself in order to respond from a more centered place.

Imagery and inner dialogue support spiritual awakening by reaching into the superconscious, uncovering inner wisdom, and releasing superconscious energies. Writing a letter to Self (chapter 3) or conversing with the Wise Being (chapter 4) may help. A letter from Self can also help us find and express wisdom we didn't know we had. For this letter, have ready a piece of paper, preferably stationery, and an envelope.

∞

Letter from Self

Close your eyes and pay attention for a moment to your breathing. Just notice the breath as it comes and goes, without trying to change it in any way. . . .

Now gently follow the breath inside your body. As you turn your attention inward, do you notice sensations of ease and pleasure anywhere in your body? Go to these places and enjoy the opening you find there. . . .

Now see if there are any parts of your body that feel tight or constricted, and imagine the sensations of ease and pleasure expanding into those places of tension or discomfort. . . .

If you need to move and adjust your position to be more comfortable, do so. Allow the sense of looseness, openness, and pleasure to slowly permeate the tissues, the muscles, the cells. . . .

You may have noticed certain feelings arising as you focused on the tightness or discomfort in your body. What are those feelings? What feelings are connected with the sensations of ease and pleasure? Let those feelings be as rich and full as they want to be, and enjoy them. . . .

Thoughts may arise as you focus on your feelings. Just notice them: those that go with the discomfort, and those that go with the ease. Gently direct your attention to the thoughts that affirm your openness and pleasure and appreciate them. . . .

These are all aspects of you—of who you are at this moment. Hold them all lightly; notice who it is that is holding them and who made the choices to direct attention to one aspect or another. . . .

Now allow yourself to step back from all that you have been holding. Move to the widest inner perspective you can discover right now—to the deepest inner place that is available to you. . . .

Let yourself imagine that you are the being who chose to be born into this lifetime, who chose to have this particular body, these feelings, this mind—who chose to be this person who is in the world. How would it be if you could remember making that choice? Let yourself drift back to that moment and be in touch again with the purpose that brought you into the world, and with the love you have for the particular form you chose. . . .

Embrace the love and wisdom and clarity that are your birthright and claim them as fully as you can right now. . . .

From this place of compassion and total acceptance, look at the person who is sitting here today, at all the turnings and choices of a lifetime that have brought this person to this moment. . . .

Is there anything you wish to say, anything you need to remind this person of? Write a letter to the person you chose to be in the world, and say what needs to be said. . . .

When you have finished the letter, put it in the envelope, seal it, and address it to yourself. Give it to a friend to mail later when it seems right to your friend to do so. It will return to you at a moment when you need to read these words and will be open to their message.

Now take some time to write in your journal about your experience in this exercise. How did your letter strike you? Did it seem wise or ordinary? Were you able to look at your personality and your life from a deeper, wider perspective? What, if anything, got in your way? Do you find any clues about how you respond to spiritual awakening, and how readily you can identify with your Self?[5]

~

OUR GROWING AND LEARNING

Spiritual awakening moves us to a more expansive context for the growing and learning. We are like snakes who must shed old skins of beliefs and habits from time to time in order to continue growing. But while we still remain within the old skin, the new experiences of awakening can be painful and confusing. We may need to face something about ourselves that we do not want to see because it is too awesome and goes against our familiar limited images of ourselves. We may be reluctant to glimpse our potential because we will also see how far we have fallen short of it.

The pain of facing our failure, our denial of the divine in ourselves and in others, may actually stop us from allowing spiritual experiences into our lives. Usually we need to go through this pain, like the pangs of childbirth, in order to continue our growth.

Frank Haronian, an "elder" in psychosynthesis, says it well:

The more one is conscious of one's positive impulses, of one's urge toward the sublime, the more shame one feels for one's failure to give expression to these impulses. There ensues a painful burning of the conscience, a sense of guilt at not being what one could be, of not doing what one could do. This is not superego guilt, but rather the cry of the Self for its actualization.[6]

The Pain of Facing Failure

I believe this pain is a major block to the collective transformation needed to sustain human life on Earth. Truly the human race has fallen short of its potential and denied the divine within. It is painful to recognize and own our collective failures. To acknowledge that we are much more wondrous and creative creatures than the images offered by mass media might mean we would have to change the way we behave! We would also be forced to acknowledge the potential greatness of the "Others"— those groups of human beings we have chosen to see as different, inferior, or wrong. We have much pain to face and go through together.

Let's practice "going through" this kind of pain in an exercise. To prepare, review your responses to the exercises "What is possible for me now in my life?" and "An ideal model," both in chapter 5.

∞

Falling Short

Take a few moments as usual to prepare yourself for inner work: breathing, relaxing, and noticing your sensations, feelings, and thoughts.

Recall times in your life when you have gone beyond your apparent limits and functioned creatively, efficiently, and energetically, times when you have accomplished something special. What qualities and skills did you possess at these times? . . .

Are not these capacities always with you? Do they give you a glimpse of what your potential may be?

Recall also your ideal model and your response to the exercise "What is possible for me now in my life?" How close are you to realizing this model and these possibilities in your everyday life? . . .

Allow yourself to consider ways you have fallen short of your potential—not so much the way you "should" be as the way you "could" be. Notice what feelings come up as you do this. . . .

Now imagine yourself expressing this potential more fully in your daily life. Think of various situations in which this might occur, with your family and friends, at work, in your community. Notice any responses, especially excuses, denial, doubts, or guilt. . . .

What underlies these responses? Let yourself experience any pain and/or sadness that is here. Breathe with it. Allow it to be here. . . .

Notice if any images or memories arise and experience the feelings that come with them. . . . Imagine your heart expanding to hold all your feelings. . . . Breathe. . . .

Stay with this experience until you feel a release, a lessening, perhaps even forgiveness. . . . Notice what happens then. . . .

What is one small step you might take to move toward your potential now? Notice your willingness to take this step. If it would be helpful, create a statement of choice and/or affirmation around this. (You may want to follow through on this choice as a Will Project, using the stages in an act of will described in chapter 9.)

Sometimes it seems that the only thing standing in the way of our greatness is our guilt and sadness at having failed in the past. John Firman calls this "existential shame and guilt" to distinguish it from toxic shame, which was discussed in chapter 7.[7] Existential shame and guilt call us to acknowledge and accept our spiritual potential. As soon as we face these feelings, we are released to move on, finding satisfying and fulfilling ways to act on who we truly are.

DOGMA AND MYSTERY

In chapter 7, we talked about the fear of not knowing and how we tend to grab hold of "truths" to make ourselves feel safe. This is particularly tempting in the spiritual arena. The mystery of the spiritual realm surpasses our theories and hypotheses. Yet we desperately want something or someone to tell us the "truth" and advise us about what to do. If we ourselves have moments of insight or if we study others who have, we may latch on to those insights for security. Spiritual insights and teachings may actually be dangerous, especially when we unquestioningly accept them as dogma.

Dogma assumes the arrogant belief that our rational minds can encompass the universe. And it exists in every field: religion, art, science, education, psychology, business, politics, and so on. When we act blindly on the basis of such dogma, we may do far more harm than good.

We can see the effects of dogma in the ecological crisis around us today. It is mankind's assumption that we know what is best for life or that what seems best for us, in the short term, is best for all. So we despoil the planet, and are often completely oblivious to the devastating effects of our actions.

When we accept information and concepts from external authority as the final truth, we may block our access to inner guidance. We may be distracted from a deeper message that lies within our own unconscious. We may suppress physical symptoms with drugs, for example, rather than heeding them as the body's messages about our mental or emotional state or need for a change in lifestyle.

Intuition as a Powerful Force

If we are able to tolerate not "knowing," and just experience what is happening—the pain and joy and whatever else—what do we discover within? In place of names, labels, and diagnoses, we may find promptings toward appropriate action and attitude. Intuition is a powerful force for guiding our lives, drawing on the deep well of our unconscious, but we all too often ignore it in favor of the usually more definite formulations of external Authority.

Another voice says, "But we can't just live on intuition all the time. That takes a level of alignment with self and concentration requiring a lot of work to achieve. It's much more efficient to use external knowledge whenever it applies, and save the inner search for the big, deep questions." A few spiritually enlightened beings may function in life without any conceptual base, without a common ground of knowledge and understanding. These beings may be able to embrace the Mystery of life and allow that unfolding revelation to guide them moment to moment.

The rest of us need understandable paradigms to guide our daily lives. And most of our paradigms work very well for us for periods of time. Our fear reaction to not knowing indicates how vitally important they are. Our challenge is to hold them loosely, always ready to revise them or let them go when we receive new information or inspiration from the world around or within.

The Scientific Method

To be open to the Mystery is, in fact, to be "scientific." In its essence, the scientific method requires that we observe without preconceptions. This is because our beliefs and concepts dramatically influence our observations of things; we tend, in fact, to "see" what fits our beliefs and ignore the rest. In any sound experimental design, even in the so-called hard sciences such as physics and chemistry, the possible effects of the human observers must be taken into account.

It is probably impossible to eliminate all preconceptions from our observations of ourselves, our lives, and our surroundings, but we can remain humble and open to change. We can at least hold any theories we have loosely, knowing they are only temporary approximations of truth that will be inevitably revised as time, and life, go on.

Attachment seems to be the key here. Concepts and "facts" we learn from others are useful as long as we don't take them as the whole and final Truth, as long as we don't hold on to them for dear life. Willingness to hang out in the Mystery and be guided from within depends on our willingness to constantly revise beliefs and theories, no matter how elegant, no matter how valuable they have been to us.

Blind Belief in Authority

I knew a young woman some years ago who was a student teacher at a school where I worked. Her parents—both teachers—had taught her that teachers were to be revered without question. This belief put her in a real quandary, because she felt inadequate to meet such a high expectation as a teacher herself. Moreover, she had trouble facing the fact that her supervising teacher had a severe drinking problem. The problem kept him home from school on many a Monday and impaired his competence as a teacher. She refused to recognize this problem—after all, he was a Teacher!—and she struggled to follow his often contradictory instructions.

This kind of blind belief in authority causes problems in other fields. Patients who believe that "the doctor always knows best" may submit themselves to inappropriate, even damaging, medical treatments. To question the doctor's recommendations would mean one would have to acknowledge that there might be no sure answers to one's medical problems. It feels more secure just to believe in the doctor's expertise.

Similarly, people believe in their spiritual leaders in cases where clear evidence exists that a leader is abusing his followers, financially or sexually. An extreme example of this occurred in Jonestown, Guiana, in 1979, when over nine hundred people committed mass suicide at the command of their spiritual leader. Such blind belief in authority—such attachment—reflects how challenging it is to struggle with the ambiguities of our complex, mysterious world.

In chapter 3, we discussed the idea of disidentification, which means that our sense of who we are is not limited to our ever-changing thoughts, feelings, physical states, and subpersonalities. We discussed Self-identification, which means connecting with the essence of our Being, Self. These concepts suggest how we can "hang out with the Mystery" and avoid the pitfalls of dogmatism by disidentifying from our beliefs and identifying with Self. The problem is that these concepts, like any others offered by psychosynthesis, can themselves become dogma and limit our growth. Even our concept of Self is, after all, only an approximation of truth.

Take a few moments to think about some precious truths which, in the past, you clung to. How did they limit your growth? How did you finally let them go? How have other people's dogmatic beliefs been a problem to you? How are dogmatic beliefs involved in some of the planetary problems we face today?

OTHER CHALLENGES OF SPIRITUAL AWAKENING

Spiritual awakening is not always comfortable. In fact, it rarely is. Change is demanded of us on many fronts, and change itself is rarely comfortable! We are plunged into the Mystery. We can never predict exactly how things will turn out. Friends and family are affected and may react in unsupportive, judgemental, fearful ways. There are pitfalls to avoid: feeling self-important or special, confusing emotional with spiritual needs, trying to escape through addictive behaviors. And perhaps, most difficult, a heightened sensitivity to suffering and violence may make life in our imperfect world seem nearly intolerable.

Do you think of yourself as being on a spiritual search right now? If you do, what are some of the challenges you are facing right now in that search? Are any of those mentioned above familiar to you, and do you have other challenges besides those?

How do we cope with all these difficulties? Answers lie within the very dilemmas we confront, for how can there be other than spiritual answers to such concerns? We seem to have no choice but to plunge into it all, opening ourselves in trust and faith to the process.

Still, there are ways we can find support and solace along the way. Meditative practices, prayer, and inspirational writings can give us glimmers of peace and hope. Rituals and ceremonies drawn from a trusted spiritual tradition, or created on our own, can lend meaning and structure to an otherwise seemingly chaotic process. Talking and spending time with friends who are struggling with their own spiritual issues remind us that we are not alone in our search; in fact, we truly are all in this together.

Take some time to think about where you find support and solace in your life. How might you find more? How might you sustain your spiritual awakening through meditation, inspirational writings, ritual, friends, and community?

Transpersonal and Spiritual Experiences

There is so much lumped under the heading of "spiritual" in today's world. Perhaps this is because we are all of us struggling toward a better relationship with the cosmos, with the sacred, with our planet, and with ourselves. We are looking for Spirit everywhere, hoping, sometimes desperately, to find an Answer to clear up our confusion and tell us how to live on our endangered Earth. And sometimes we are simply looking for an easy way out!

We have so many paths and ways to choose from now, ancient and modern, Eastern and Western. We can consult various versions of the tarot, the *I Ching,* the runes, and our astrological chart. We can study with spiritual teachers from every world religion and many syntheses. We can seek guidance from those who channel wisdom from other realms and entities. And we can, as always, seek within ourselves through prayer, meditation, imagination, and reason.

Unfortunately, there are many people in our world ready to take advantage of our desperation, ready to provide us with easy answers, emotional highs, and a defined path to follow. Often these "paths" take us "into ourselves" at the expense of the larger world. Although they use the trappings of spirituality, they may actually be worshiping the false gods of egotism and greed.

There are other people who have found answers that satisfy them, at least for a while; sometimes they look for converts to support them in their convictions. If we follow some of these people for a while and discover their all too human failings—or worse, are betrayed by their grasping for wealth and power—we may feel mistrustful of all so-called spiritual paths.

Two Kinds of Spirituality

One way we can make sense of all this is to distinguish between two kinds of "spirituality"—one we would label "transpersonal" and the other "spiritual." Into the transpersonal category, we will put all the paths that help us connect with our superconscious, our potential, our wisdom, and other transpersonal qualities. We will reserve the spiritual category for the more ineffable experiences of the Divine, and the sacred responsibility and choices that such experiences impress upon us.[8] Each person must, of course, be the judge of the nature of his or her own experiences.

Most—possibly all—of the exercises included in this book fall into the realms of personal and transpersonal psychosynthesis. I think it would be very presumptuous of me to imagine that I could compose an exercise or guided meditation to evoke a direct experience of Self. Even the letters to and from Self probably tap only into our superconscious most of the time. And these exercises are deliberately open-ended; I do not presume to guide you through such a dialogue, at least not in any standardized form. If someone does have a truly spiritual experience as a result of any exercise in this book, it is through grace, not through any direct agency of mine or of "psychosynthesis" as a system. Such experiences are always available to us; we need only to clear away the debris and awaken to them.

To quote Roberto Assagioli, "Psychosynthesis does not aim or attempt to give a metaphysical nor a theological explanation of the great Mystery—it leads to the door, but stops there."[9]

Equally Valid Experiences

Lest I seem to set one kind of experience above another, let me hasten to say that the transpersonal and spiritual experiences are equally valid and valuable in our wholeness. Experiences of either kind support our growth and development, and our effectiveness in the world. Self underlies all our life experiences anyway, whether they be pleasant or unpleasant, joyful or tragic, personal, transpersonal, or spiritual.

I believe it is helpful to discriminate between these kinds of experiences, however, so that our realization of Self is not confused with the forms and words—the contents—of the paths mentioned above. Our relationship with Self is sacred and private; although we may learn wisdom and practices from studying with a teacher or by following a particular discipline, it is ultimately up to each of us to find and follow our own truth. We need to be wary of anyone or any system that attempts to intrude into that sacred place.

CREATIVE MEDITATION

Meditation is a reliable and powerful path to the transpersonal realms, and sometimes to the spiritual. We discussed earlier the value of meditation in centering and self-awareness. There are many meditative approaches, too many and too subtle to try to outline here. I want to introduce only one approach because it has been most closely associated with psychosynthesis and was taught to me by Assagioli when my husband and I studied with him in 1973. I found it a powerful training for other forms of meditation, for it helped me learn to concentrate and direct my mind. This approach also helped me study and bring into my life various transpersonal qualities that were the focus of my meditation over the first few years.

Creative meditation, as it is called, is based on raja yoga, a mind-training yoga from the Hindu tradition. In this approach, one focuses on a particular quality, phrase, or "seed thought," working through three stages: reflective, receptive, and creative. These stages are described below so that you can experience and practice them for yourself.

∞

1. Reflective Meditation

Begin by closing your eyes and paying attention to your breath, as usual. Allow concerns and worries to fall away for the moment, and simply observe your breathing, your body sensations, your feelings and thoughts.

When you feel ready, consider what you would like to have as the focus of this meditation: a quality you would like to bring into your life more, a short phrase from a poem or sacred writings, a word arising from your unconscious. Take a few moments to choose your focus now.

Now write your quality, word, or phrase in a small circle in the center of a blank sheet of paper. On imaginary lines radiating out from the circle, begin to write words or very short phrases that you associate with the quality named in the circle. Include synonyms, opposites, associated qualities, feelings, people you think have this quality, and so on. There are no rules to limit what you write, only the space available. (For example, if I wrote "serenity" in the circle, I might write the following words radiating out from the circle: peace, quiet, unperturbable, longing, boring, no adventure, upset, happiness, clarity . . .)

When you have filled the page, or run out of words, take a look at what you have written, and see if you can identify any particular patterns or categories. Notice what surprised you and what was new.

Reflect on the literal meaning of your seed thought. Look up the words in a dictionary, if possible, one that shows the roots of words.

How have you experienced this quality or truth in your life? Who exemplifies this quality or truth to you—someone you know personally, or someone you have heard or read about? How would your life be changed if you were to bring this quality or truth into greater manifestation? How would it affect those around you?

What gets in the way of your bringing this more into your life?

How would the world be changed if more people knew and acted on this truth or from this quality? What gets in the way of that happening?

What is the source of this quality or truth? How or where do you find it in yourself or in the world?

What other thoughts and questions have you about this quality or truth?

When you feel finished with this stage or when you have gone as far as you can for now, return to your breathing and prepare for the next stage.

2. Receptive Meditation

Take some time to settle into yourself, into silence and peacefulness. Notice any feelings that have been aroused by the reflective process and let them gradually subside.

Now imagine gathering up all the thoughts, images, ideas, insights, and feelings from your reflections on your seed thought. Imagine holding them all in a beautiful container, a bowl or basket or whatever. Then imagine holding this container up to the light of the sun, to let its rays shine upon all that is there.

Let the sunlight pour down upon you as well. Imagine your mind like a lake, unruffled by the wind, deep, clear, and mirror-like, reflecting all that lies around it.

Now you must wait, receptive to any further understanding or insight that will come. Notice any thoughts, feelings, and sensations that arise and let them gently pass by. Return to your expectant and patient watch. . . .

If inspiration occurs, either dramatic or subtle, breathe into the experience. Give it time to flower. Notice your feelings and thoughts in response. . . . Then, when you are ready, make some notes or a drawing to remind you of what you received.

If nothing comes, wait a little longer. Notice any impatience or fear you feel. Breathe. Acknowledge the difficulty of this kind of patient receptivity, how different it is from our usual mode of thinking and acting. Breathe again.

When you decide to end this stage, affirm to yourself the possibility of receiving more understanding and insight at a later time, from something you hear or read, from your dreams or journaling, or during another meditation. Inspiration may come from surprising places once you have opened yourself to it through this practice.

3. Creative Meditation

Begin this stage by breathing, relaxing, and observing your sensations, feelings, and thoughts. . . . When you feel ready, recall the major insights you had in the reflective and receptive stages.

Now imagine how your life would be different if you acted on these insights. Imagine yourself in various daily situations and notice any differences these insights seem to make in how you feel, how you see the world, how you act. . . .

Now imagine the effects of this insight rippling out into your community, region, country, and throughout the world. How might this understanding transform the world? Let your imagination play with this idea, presenting various scenes to your inner eye, ear, and senses. . . . Make some notes when you feel finished.

∞

Each stage of this meditative process exercises important faculties. The reflective stage helps us develop our thinking mind, our "reason," and our capacity to put together various bits of information and ideas into useful patterns. It makes use of our imagination and emotions as well. The receptive stage teaches us to go beyond our conscious mind, to allow our unconscious mind to work as well, and to open ourselves to inspiration from the superconscious, and perhaps from Self and Spirit. The creative stage directs the power of our mind toward transformation, toward manifesting our vision. As many wise teachers have said, we can only go as far as our imaginations reach.

All together, the three stages teach discipline, concentration, and trust in the miraculous capacities of our minds.

COMING TO TERMS WITH THE WORLD-AS-IT-IS

One of the most difficult spiritual challenges we face, have faced, or ever will face, is making peace with a world of impermanence, change, loss, violence, cruelty, suffering, and injustice. All great religions have struggled with this problem; it may be at the heart of all spiritual/religious searching. Obviously, I will not claim to have a solution to this dilemma. I can only offer some thoughts and suggest a process that may help you on your own quest.

What do you find difficult to accept about the world or about life? What recent tragedies—earthquakes, hurricanes, fires, wars, crimes of violence, famines, or floods—have challenged your capacities to accept and affirm life? You may recall that we explored this dilemma in chapter 2, in the context of accepting our personal existential reality. Remember that acceptance does not mean resignation or even approval; we do not have to give up our desire for change. Acceptance is simply a realistic recognition of things being the way they are and a willingness to work from there. And realistically, our world is full of enormous horror and suffering, as well as bountiful goodness and joy.

The Creative Meditation process outlined in this chapter can be used to come to terms with the world-as-it-is. Choose for your seed thought a quality such as equanimity, serenity, or acceptance. Or choose a short passage from poetry or inspirational writing that addresses this dilemma, perhaps a verse from the Bible or a sentence from Buddhist scripture. Over time, your meditation will open you to deeper truths and larger perspectives; the attention you give them will enable the qualities you contemplate to grow within you.

An Affirmation of Acceptance

Try writing an affirmation for yourself out of your meditation to use as a daily dedication or to remind yourself of your commitment to accepting the world-as-it-is. Here is one I wrote for myself not long ago:

> I choose to accept the world just as it is. I choose life on this planet, in this world, at this time. I choose to accept the pain I feel when I witness violence, and the joy I feel when I witness love. I let go of the demand that the world live up to my expectations and values while I dedicate myself to sharing love and light with all.

As tough as they are to contemplate, I have also found helpful the "Five Remembrances" of Buddhism, as translated by Thich Nhat Hanh in the *Plum Village Chanting Book*.[10] The

Five Remembrances confront the things we human beings most fear. In many Buddhist traditions, they are recited on a daily basis to help the practitioner develop equanimity in the face of the incontrovertible truths of aging, ill health, death, and impermanence. The Five Remembrances are usually recited in a meditative setting, interspersed by the sound of a bell and a brief period of silence. (I have slightly adapted #4.)

1. I am of the nature to grow old. There is no way to escape growing old.
2. I am of the nature to have ill health. There is no way to escape having ill health.
3. I am of the nature to die. There is no way to escape death.
4. All that is dear to me and everyone I love are of the nature to change. There is no way to escape [their changing].
5. My actions are my only true belongings. I cannot escape the consequences of my actions. My actions are the ground on which I stand.

Coming to terms with the world-as-it-is has led me to a growing conviction that we are in a time of crisis, a time of dangerous opportunity. We may indeed destroy ourselves as a species and do long-lasting harm to all living beings on Earth. Or, equally possible, we may awaken to our folly and discover how to live in harmony with the Earth. The crises we see around us are the alarm bells we need to awaken. Will we heed them in time?

A GREAT SPIRITUAL AWAKENING MAY BE HAPPENING

We don't have to look far to see evidence that a great collective spiritual awakening may be already upon us. People are discovering their collective power and throwing off oppressive regimes around the world, often nonviolently, from the Philippines to Eastern Europe and the republics of the former Soviet Union. People all over the world are organizing to protect their rivers, lakes, wetlands, forests, mountains, and other natural resources. These are signs of a shift in consciousness and values, a shift that is spiritual at its heart, because it has to do with our interrelatedness and responsibility to the commonweal.

Of course, at the same time, there seems to be evidence to the contrary. The overwhelming support of the American people for the 1991 Persian Gulf war and the nationalism that followed might be interpreted as strengthening separatism in some of its forms: racism, fascism, classism. However, many Americans sincerely believed we had no moral choice but to rescue the Kuwaitis from a "mad-dog dictator." Thus the widespread support for the war may have been more a result of our lack of understanding about Middle Eastern culture and history than of our spiritual deficiency as a people. In our desire for a simple "truth" behind which we could rally, we may have supported an overly simplistic solution at the cost of many lives and great environmental damage.

New Opportunities

Each day we are offered new opportunities to awaken, to unite in compassion and caring with our fellow human beings, to evaluate our mistakes and change our ways. Natural and human-made disasters such as earthquakes, hurricanes, fires, and urban riots leave us trying to understand how such things can happen so suddenly, come to terms with our powerlessness, help the victims recover, and evaluate the errors that were made before and during the disaster. There are usually even deeper lessons to be learned from such tragedies.

Spiritual awakening may seem to happen within the confines of the individual human heart and mind, but in reality, it happens to all of us together. Each person who finds a spark of light within cannot help sharing it with others. Public events, as much as private ones, challenge and impact each of us spiritually, although we may be largely unaware of their effects. We try to separate ourselves, one from another, at the peril of our very survival. We must each and all take responsibility for the fate of our world. And there is no one but us. There never has been.

11. *Relationships: Growing Whole Together*

The Sun Dancer believes that each person is a unique Living Medicine Wheel, powerful beyond imagination, that has been limited and placed upon this earth to Touch, Experience and Learn. The Six Grandfathers Taught me that each man, woman, and child at one time was a Living Power that existed somewhere in time and space. These Powers were without form, but they were aware. They were alive.

Each Power possessed boundless energy and beauty. These Living Medicine Wheels were capable of nearly anything. They were perfect in all ways except one. They had no understanding of limitation, no experience of substance. These Beings were total energy of the Mind, without Body or Heart. They were placed upon this earth that they might Learn the things of the Heart through Touching.

According to the Teachers, there is only one thing that all people possess equally. This is their loneliness. No two people on the face of the earth are alike in any one thing except for their loneliness. This is the cause of our Growing, but it is also the cause of our wars. Love, hate, greed and generosity are all rooted within our loneliness, within our desire to be needed and loved.

The only way we can overcome our loneliness is through Touching. It is only in this way that we can learn to be Total Beings. God is a presence of this Total... this Wholeness. [1]

—Hyemeyohsts Storm

WE HAVE FOCUSED until now on individual work, on how we as individuals can discover our inner wealth and bring it more into our daily life. So a chapter on relationships might seem to be a bit of a departure. Actually, we have been working with relationships all along: the relationship of the various aspects of the personality to one another, and to the whole, and the relationship of this whole to Self and Spirit, and to the interconnected web of life that contains us all. Our journey of Self-discovery and Self-realization has been in the context of our desire to make a difference in the world, so we have been working in relationship to our families, communities, and the environment. Our relationships are laboratories for our spiritual growth and awakening.

A PSYCHOSYNTHESIS OVERVIEW

Now we look at our relationships to others more specifically. This is obviously a huge topic, worthy of a book unto itself. We will limit our exploration here to an overview of a psychosynthesis approach to relationships, with a few exercises to deepen the experience. In the process, we will at least touch on these questions: What is love? How do we balance individuality with mutuality? How can we grow through our relationships with lovers and life partners? How can we create loving, supportive, and respectful relationships with our children? What constitutes a healthy relationship with our community, our nation, the whole human family? How can we deepen our experience of relationship with nature and with other living beings, including the Earth itself?

Systems theory has helped us to see everything as part of larger wholes; everything is in relationship to everything else. When we try to define ourselves as separate, we run into trouble. Although we may believe we are isolated, especially if we are living alone and are not involved in a "primary relationship," we cannot escape being in relationship to our communities and our natural environment. Like it or not, we are in relationship with the other people on the bus, with the homeless people on the street, with the grocery clerk and the letter carrier. Any contact we have with mass media—newspapers, magazines, television, or radio—puts us in relationship with the culture around us. Even more basically, we breathe air, which is shared with all the living beings around us, and which may carry particles from dust storms, fires, or volcanoes thousands of miles away.

And we are truly "in" relationship; relationship contains us, sustains us, keeps us alive. As Joanna Macy so eloquently puts it: "It is the web of life in which you have taken being and in which you are supported. Out of that vast web you cannot fall."[2]

∞

Web of Relationships

Take a few moments to contemplate the vast web of relationships that support you. Make note of a few of your biological, economic, political, social, cultural, spiritual, professional, familial, close, and intimate relationships.

Now breathe quietly for several minutes, letting your breath deepen your sense of these relationships and noticing any feelings which come up.

How have these various relationships given you support, nurture, help? How have they injured or betrayed you? How have you learned from them?

∞

We have all been wounded in relationships—betrayed, rejected, exploited, even brutalized. As a result, we are sometimes suspicious, hard-hearted, or manipulative in our response to others. Our mutual wounding is enormous and is at the heart of all our human conflicts. Yet we cannot survive without each other, and we are driven by our deep need to connect with one another. We really have no choice but to love.

Love Binds Us Together

Ferrucci retells a story by Tolstoy about a fallen angel who must learn what people live by in order to return to heaven. Finally he realizes "that human beings cannot live each for himself, that they are necessary to one another, and that love is what they live by."[3] Ferrucci goes on to speculate that "the yearning for unity seems to be present even in the most elementary forms of life. It may be something analogous to that deeply rooted need, that obscure nostalgia for undifferentiated oneness, that sense of belonging and inclusiveness, which appears in numerous forms and to which we sometimes give the name of 'love.'" [4]

In its broadest sense, love is the force of unconditional attraction which binds us all together, which binds together everything in the universe. We are all interconnected through this underlying force, no matter how we may feel about each other. So all relationships ultimately are based on love, however unconscious and distorted it may be. Our basic challenge in any relationship may be to discover the underlying connection-attraction-unity-love and be guided thereby in our actions within that relationship.

That's a pretty tall order for anyone. It's hard for me to get in touch with our underlying unity when someone has just insulted or attacked me. I might be afraid that such a perspective would prevent me from protecting myself and my integrity. Unity and love are all too often misconstrued to mean I must sacrifice my own self-interest to indulge the whims or demands of another, or that I must lose my personal identity and individuality in some kind of amorphous love soup. These are both gross distortions of what love and unity mean.

First of all, our underlying unity doesn't mean it's okay for anyone to harm another, or for us to allow another to harm us. As a matter of fact, such behavior is unloving and divisive and needs to be countered in the interests of love and unity. Actually, we honor our essential unity when we say no to another's harmful behavior.

Moreover, our underlying unity and love demand that we respect individual boundaries and differences. There is a kind of paradox in this: love and unity are meaningless words if we have no separations or differences from one another. Hyemeyohsts Storm speaks to this paradox in his recounting of the Plains Indian Teaching that began this chapter. We need boundaries, separations, and differences in order to learn "the things of the Heart" through Touching.

DYNAMICS OF HEALTHY RELATIONSHIPS

Love may be the binding force of the universe, but in everyday life, the skills for being in relationship don't seem to come automatically. In fact, much of our current social conditioning seems to work against healthy relationships, teaching us to separate and compete, rather than to commune and cooperate. It isn't only a matter of changing our perspective from suspicion to love; it is also a matter of changing old beliefs and habits of behavior from defensive to connecting.

179

The dynamics of healthy relationships are complex. Relationship demands involvement, honesty, empathy, acceptance, and respect. It requires clear, yet flexible, boundaries between you and me, your needs and mine. We each have to discover who we are as distinct from one another, as well as how we are the same. We need sensitivity about how and when we project feelings, points of view, and judgements on one another. We need to allow for our expectations of one another at the same time that we learn to keep them minimal and realistic.

All this means we need to have good communication skills, to listen deeply to hear the feelings behind the words, and to express clearly what we feel and think, want and need. We need conflict resolution skills that serve the interests and needs of all parties. Then we can seek solutions to our mutual dilemmas without there being any losers.

These skills come easier when our basic attitude is positive, open, and loving, when we approach interactions with others with confidence and clarity. It comes back to more work on ourselves; relationships challenge us repeatedly to face ourselves and to discover what patterns within our own psyches are blocking our ability to connect and to love.

∞

Looking in a Relationship Mirror

Choose one relationship that you would like to improve. Think about it, your history with this person, and the problems that come between you. . . .

What behaviors of the other person bother you the most?

How do you feel when the other person behaves this way? Try to identify your feelings (not thoughts or judgements) very specifically. . . .

As you get more in touch with your feelings, you may recognize a subpersonality, a familiar pattern that you also experience in other relationships. Let an image emerge for the feelings, or for the subpersonality, that feels this way. You may want to draw it in your journal. . . .

Now talk with this image, asking it what it wants, and doesn't want, and more about how it feels. Find out as much as you can about it, how old it is, its name, and so forth. . . .

What does this subpersonality really, really need? Take some time to sense this, so that your answer comes from your inner "knowing" and not only from your logical mind. . . .

Imagine that you can give this part what it needs, that you have the capacity to meet its need. Perhaps you can imagine using a symbolic object to represent your gift. How does your subpersonality receive your gift? How does it change?

Now ask this part of you what it has to offer to the relationship in question. What quality or gift does it have to contribute to the relationship with the other person? Imagine this quality or gift being expressed in the relationship, and see what changes. . . .

You may need to make some agreements for the future with your subpersonality. Take some time to complete your conversation with this part, and then bring it back inside yourself in some way. Make notes in your journal if you wish.

We are working on the assumption that many of our reactions to other people's behavior are based on our own unresolved feelings and needs. When we can identify our feelings and needs and take care of them ourselves, we are free to meet the other person without preconditions. We can accept others on their own terms without expecting them to take care of our feelings and needs.

A process like this might lead to a decision to talk with the other person about your feelings and needs. That is entirely appropriate in friendships and intimate partnerships. It may even be appropriate in some professional relationships. The purpose of such a conversation would be to create more understanding between you and another person. Such understanding might prompt the other person to change his or her behavior toward you in order to support your needs. Expecting that result, however, would put the responsibility back on the other person and probably lead to more tension.

We Must First Reassure Ourselves

For example, in exploring my relationship with my husband, I might identify an insecure little girl who wants reassurance that she is loved. I might see that she is left over from my childhood. In the dialogue in the exercise, I would take responsibility for giving her this reassurance myself. I might discover in the process that her vulnerability is a valuable quality to bring to the relationship with my husband. I probably would want to share these insights with him so that he would understand my demanding behaviors.

However, if I then expected him to reassure me of his love all the time, I would be putting this little girl in his hands, and she is not his responsibility; she is mine! It is up to me to help her to feel loved; I need to love her first of all! If I don't, she probably won't be satisfied with his reassurances anyway, no matter how frequent or passionate. Besides, he has his own insecure little boy to take care of; he doesn't need to take on my little girl as well.

Nevertheless, he might respond to my sharing by reaching out more, by being more reassuring. I might even ask him to express his love to me more often in certain ways, or in certain circumstances in which the little girl is more likely to come out. I might say, "I'm feeling real insecure right now; would you tell me you love me or give me a hug?" Notice how different that is from "Why don't you ever tell me you love me?" which carries a not-so-subtle accusation. There is nothing wrong with our asking close friends and partners to help meet our inner needs; this is part of the way we can take care of ourselves. But the primary responsibility must remain within each of us.

A Powerful Approach

Working with subpersonalities is a powerful approach to improving relationships. This is because we are often in relationship through our subpersonalities. One of my subpersonalities is like a stereotyped "Governess," strict and controlling. If I interact with someone else in this pattern, the other person may react like a rebellious child. When this happens, we may get into a vicious circle that is difficult to escape, unless one or both of us is able to disidentify from our subpersonality and step into a wider perspective. Systems theory tells us that change in any part of a system always affects the whole, since all the other parts respond to that change. That is why work on ourselves can transform a relationship without the other person's consciously initiating any change.

It is often easier to recognize someone else's subpersonality than to recognize our own, and this can provide a useful perspective. When I imagine that another's behavior is coming from a subpersonality, I am less likely to throw out the baby with the bathwater. I may be more patient, just waiting until the other person regains center, or I may be able to respond to the subpersonality's underlying need. In either case, I am likely to be a little more forgiving, just as I hope to be forgiven when I act unconsciously from one of my less desirable sub-personalities.

∞

Subpersonalities in Relationship

Take a few minutes to think about someone with whom you have a close relationship. This could be the person you used in the last exercise, or someone else. What are some of this person's behaviors or moods that trouble you?

Imagine that these behaviors and moods represent sub-personalities. How would you describe these subpersonalities? You may want to give them names. . . .

Now choose one, and imagine that you could engage in a dialogue with this subpersonality, as if it were your own. What might it have to say about its wants and feelings?

What might be its underlying need?

What might it have to offer to the other person? To you?

What subpersonalities of yours tend to get involved with this one? Have you any insights about their common needs and gifts? How might you help them work (and play) together?

Now recall a situation in which the other person acted from this subpersonality. Notice if you feel differently about it now. How might you respond now with your new insights?

∞

RESPONSE-ABILITY

Working with subpersonalities in this way assumes a rea-sonably positive relationship in which the two people love and respect each other and wish to support one another. There obviously are relationships in which the other's behavior is destructive and hurtful, so working on one's own attitudes may not be enough. A process such as the one in the last exercise may help to make this clear. In such situations, the subpersonality discovered may need safety, and in order to provide it safety, one may need to demand a change in the other person's behavior, to limit the relationship, even to end it. The responsibility remains in one's own hands. When we are the victims of another's abuse, it is still up to us to take care of ourselves.

Remember the work we did with anger in chapter 7? The process of transforming anger to power is vital to healthy relationships. When another's behavior is actively hurtful to us, or is contrary to our deepest values, we have to make some choices about how we want to respond. By working through the anger process, we identify and affirm our value, and may be able to let go of the demand that the other person live up to our values. And we may choose to change the nature of our relationship to that other person.

For example, if someone were to physically or verbally attack me or anyone else in my presence, I would object and intervene (or at least that is my intention.) It would be a violation of my commitment to nonviolence to tolerate violence within my sphere of influence. If the abuse or violence continued or recurred, I would take whatever measures were necessary to stop it. If I were the object, I would limit or end the relationship. If someone else were the victim, I would help that person to get out of the situation. In extreme circumstances, I would seek help from the police or the courts.

Each Part Affects the Whole

Systems theory teaches that changes to any part are reflected in every other part and therefore in the whole system.

So damage to any part damages every other part, and the whole. When someone injures another person, including me, that injury will be reflected throughout the social system in which we are involved. On the other hand, if I take steps to stop the abusive behavior, I protect the well-being of the whole system—which, of course, includes the abusive person.

In a sense, we are all responsible for our collective health and morality—responsible in the sense that we have the *ability to respond*. We often forget that we have this ability, and our forgetfulness can last for extended periods of time. We become identified with helpless, frightened subpersonalities, reverting to a time when we truly were helpless, frightened children. We get caught up in the systems of attitude around us, forgetting that change can come into a system through any part—through each of us. We compromise our values to conform to what everyone else is doing. And if we do take "responsibility," it may be in the form of self-blame and guilt, further crippling ourselves in taking appropriate action. Another vicious circle!

We Can Choose

When we awaken to our ability to choose, when we remember that we have a will, we can escape from these prisons and seek our field of freedom within the constraints of the situation. There is almost always some action we can take, however subtle and small it may seem. It might be as simple as a smile, a nod, an outstretched hand. It might be as subtle as a shift in perspective inside our own minds. We can open our hearts and at the same time set limits to the behavior we will tolerate from others. And we can nearly always offer comfort and a listening ear to those who are suffering from abuse. All of these actions will be reflected throughout the system, subtly and certainly facilitating transformation.

In thinking about our interactions in relationships, we tend to use the language and patterns of cause and effect. "I did this and so he did that." This can lead to guilt, recriminations, and blame. "If I had only done thus-and-so, everything would have been better." "When she did such-and-such, I had no choice but to do what I did." This kind of thinking glosses over the real subtleties and complexities of human interaction.

We Each Have an Effect

System theorists try to point us in another direction, to help us think in terms of "mutual causality" or of "dependent co-arising," to use Joanna Macy's terms.[5] We all "cause" situations together, in the moment, interacting with the forces of nature and coincidence. Although everything we do affects what happens, no single action or person can rightfully claim either full credit or blame. This is such a major shift in Western thought that it is very difficult for most of us to really grasp the implications. Nevertheless, this perspective promises to free us from guilt and helplessness and to enable us to transform ourselves and our society, so it makes sense to at least try it on for size.[6] Let's look at a "loaded" relationship situation from this perspective.

⊙

Responding to Hurtful Behavior

Recall an incident in your adult life when you responded effectively to someone's hurtful behavior, whether you or someone else was the target. Run the incident through your mind as if watching a film, and review what happened as accurately as you can. . . .

What were your feelings and thoughts? How did you respond or react?

What helped you respond in the way you did?

How was your response reflected in the other people's behavior and in the whole situation?

How were you changed by the experience; what did you learn?

⊗

Many years ago, my husband and I were living in married student housing with our two small children. Our four-year-old befriended a four-year-old next door, and I became friends with his mother. She and her husband were having marital problems, which culminated in his moving out. For more than two weeks, he did not visit or contact his son, in spite of the mother's attempts to communicate to him about the situation.

At first, I felt fairly helpless to do anything, partly because I didn't know the father very well, and partly because I had been taught to "mind my own business." My concern for the boy finally overcame my reluctance, and I wrote the father a note, telling him how much distress his son was in and urging him to not neglect his son just because he was angry with his wife.

A couple of days later, the father came to take his son for an outing and apparently continued to visit with him regularly. Had the father been even more emotionally cut off from his son, my letter might have done no good, or might have even made him angrier. But I had to try and fortunately, it worked.

"Minding my own business" has sometimes inhibited me from action when I have observed people mistreating their children in public. I have come to believe, however, that when the welfare of children is at stake, it is the business of everyone in the community. Even believing this, I often can't think of what to say or do, because I am paralyzed by my fear of incurring the other person's wrath. I may make the excuse to myself that nothing I could do would help anyway. But when I act, I always feel better about myself, no matter what the apparent result. And I can never predict how what I say or do may subtly influence the person, especially if he or she receives similar responses from others.

THE SYNTHESIS OF THE COUPLE

Many of us find our greatest challenges in a relationship with a primary life partner. If we are fortunate, this relationship also brings us love, support, fulfillment, and security. We tend to expect more from such a relationship, to project more onto our partner than onto anyone else. We may experience a wider—and wilder—range of feelings in this relationship than any other, save possibly that with our children. We can certainly learn a great deal from such a relationship, and what we learn carries over into every other relationship in our lives.

Assagioli offered a model for couple relationships which he called "the synthesis of the couple." He used a triangle to represent the dynamics, as shown in figure 3, page 190.[7] The points at the ends of the base of the triangle represent two members of the couple. The apex of the triangle represents the purpose of the relationship, a unifying focus for both partners.

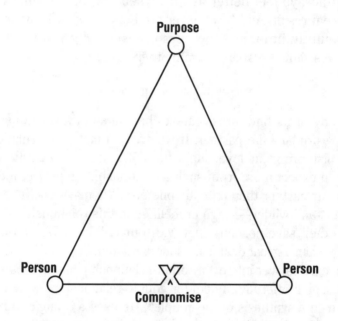

Figure 3 – Synthesis of the Couple triangle model

When the two partners are focused primarily on what they need and want from one another, they are relating along the baseline of the triangle. If there is a conflict, they must meet somewhere along that line, and any resolution to that conflict can come only from compromise, meaning that each gives up something in order to reach agreement. And one may give up more than the other. This point of compromise is represented by the X on the baseline.

If, however, the couple relate to each other within the context of their higher purpose as a couple, represented by the apex, then synthesis is possible. Synthesis means that the essence of each person's needs and values is recognized and included. No one gives up anything essential; no one loses. The resolution of any conflict comes from viewing the conflict from a broader and unifying perspective, rather than from the more limited perspective of "my needs versus yours."

THE ELLIPSE

Another model for representing this kind of synthesis was proposed to me recently by Robert Kimball, a theologian at Starr King School for the Ministry in Berkeley, California. He suggests an ellipse with two centers, one representing each person, and the ellipse representing the Larger Whole, which is created by the commitment of the couple to a common sense of purpose, as well as to each other (see figure 4 on the next page). I think this model conveys more clearly the quality of *inclusiveness*. The synthesis of the couple does not exist outside them, but rather carries them both, with their full individuality, within its embrace.

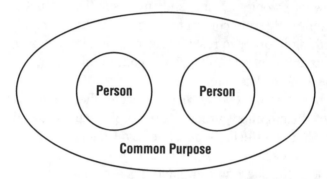

Figure 4 – Synthesis of the Couple alternative model

The broader unifying focus or purpose of a relationship may be profound or prosaic. Some couples find their unifying purpose in raising their children; when their children are grown, they may suffer from alienation and conflict if they have not discovered another purpose. Other couples have a common work: building a house, a family business, or closely related professions. The common purpose may be to support one another's personal and professional growth. It may lie in common values or religious convictions. There are probably as many purposes for couples as there are couples; what matters is that this purpose be recognized and valued, and that decisions be made and conflicts resolved within this context.

∽

Exploring a Relationship

If you are in a primary relationship, or in the process of developing one, take a few minutes now to consider how you relate to one another and what holds you together as a couple or what attracts you to the relationship.

What are your needs and wants from the other person? What happens when he or she fails to meet your needs?

What are the other person's needs and wants from you? What happens when you fail to meet them?

Next is a drawing, so get out your crayons or pastels, and drawing paper or journal. Take a few minutes now to go inside, relax, and breathe. . . .

Imagine that you can hold the relationship as a whole in your awareness, experiencing its many facets, complexities, and dynamics without analysis. Take some time to review its history and its current qualities. Then allow an image to emerge for your experience of this relationship, as it is right now, and sketch it on your paper. . . .

Notice any feelings or insights and make some notes about them.

Now take a few deep breaths, and let this image move into the background. Return to your quiet place inside. When you are ready, ask the question: *What is our purpose as a couple?* Notice any sensations, sounds, or visual images that come up in response. Observe them for a while and then record them in a drawing.

Notice and make notes about any feelings or insights from this drawing.

It may be helpful to also do some free writing on the question *What is our purpose as a couple?* Set a time for yourself of at least ten minutes and write continuously during that time, without regard for spelling, complete sentences, or even "making sense."

Again, return to a quiet place inside, and breathe. Continue to "hold" your experience of your relationship in your awareness, and then ask, *What gets in the way of our purpose as a couple?* Consider roadblocks that you each create, as well as those you create together. . . .

Returning inside and breathing, ask, *What qualities do we need to develop that would help us move through these blocks and realize our purpose as a couple?*

Finally, return within and ask, *What qualities do I need to develop?* Make notes about your inner responses.

Although it is very interesting and useful for both members of a couple to do this exercise and compare notes, it is by no means necessary. The insights gained about how you are "holding" the relationship can create a whole new perspective and open up new options for your actions, even without your partner's participation.

If, however, your conclusions from this exercise are fairly drastic, such as "There is no purpose in our relationship and I should end it!" be sure to check out your conclusions with your partner, or a counselor, therapist, or close trusted friend. Because our feelings in primary relationships run so high, we can sometimes go off the deep end and need external feedback to help us see the bigger picture. Your drastic conclusions may be appropriate; checking them out will only strengthen them if this is the case.

On the other hand, you might have a beautiful vision of the purpose of your relationship but find seemingly insurmountable obstacles to fulfilling that purpose. It may be that your vision of the purpose is idealized and unrealistic. Or it may be that you both have a lot of work to do, separately and together.

Let the vision of your purpose energize your common work on your communication, on your expectations of each other, and on your individual "baggage" from the past. Consider seeking marriage counseling or individual therapy. Primary relationships are too valuable to set aside because counseling seems too painful, scary, or expensive.

THE SELF OF THE COUPLE

Envisioning the purpose of a relationship is a way of aligning the relationship with Self. When two people come together in relationship, it is as if their Selves come together to create the Self of the couple, a Source of guidance for both members.

It is difficult to find the words to describe this concept, because it is so hard to describe or define Self; to talk about two "Selves" joining in some way sounds as if they were previously separate. That would seem to contradict our understanding of Self as being at once individual and unified with everything. We all connect with each other through Self, so perhaps all we are saying here is that we can call upon this Source in a specific relationship, as well as for ourselves as individuals.

At any rate, the notion that a coherent Force embraces a relationship—providing sustenance, learning, and healing for both partners—is powerful. The notion alone can help us keep the faith during the hard times. Maybe this is what is meant by the old saying "a marriage made in heaven." Conceiving of a spiritual Will behind a relationship can certainly motivate one to take a second look, go deeper into the heart of conflicts, and hold the difficulties in a more positive light.

Let's imagine that you can converse with this Couple Self (or at least its representative) about an issue in your relationship.

This kind of journey through imagery can be done with both partners participating, both sharing their images and visions in turn as they go along. It is not necessary for both partners to agree about various events; one partner could, for example, envision the Being as an old man, while the other envisions two young angels, male and female. Simply allow the two versions to unfold together, noticing similarities and differences with interest and acceptance. The richness, diversity, and complementarity of the partnership will be evident, along with areas of discord.

∞

A Couple's Journey

Prepare yourself in the usual way to go on an inner journey: close your eyes, breathe, and allow your body, feelings, and mind to quiet. . . .

Imagine yourself in a meadow with your partner. Take time to experience the sights, sounds, and sensations of the meadow. . . . Notice how it feels to be there with your partner and how each of you responds to the meadow and each other. . . .

Look around the meadow and find a path that leads into the forest and up the side of a mountain nearby. When you find it, begin to walk along it with your partner. Notice how you walk, your relationship to each other, and what the path is like. . . . After you have hiked for a while, you may want to pause and make some notes about what has happened so far. . . .

As you resume walking, notice how near you are to the top of the mountain. Notice if the going is easier or more difficult as you climb. . . .

Imagine that you are close to the top. . . . Now imagine that you have arrived at the top of the mountain with your partner. Take time to look around. Imagine talking with your partner about the experience so far. . . .

You will notice a small building in the distance. This is the home of very Wise Beings who have much to teach you about your relationship. Walk toward the building together and see if the Beings appear; there might be one or two Beings, or more. Perhaps they will come out of the building and greet you, or perhaps you will need to knock on their door and ask them to come out. Just allow whatever happens. . . .

Take time to just experience the presence of the Being(s) before you. Notice and enjoy whatever qualities she/he/they possess: love, wisdom, compassion, acceptance. . . .

Now begin your conversation by asking questions and/or by opening up to what the Being(s) may have to say. Take all the time you need, asking more questions, sharing feelings, and so on. . . . Give both yourself and your partner a chance to talk. Pause to take notes if you wish. . . .

The Being(s) may have a gift to offer the two of you or one for each of you. What do you receive? How do you respond to the gift?

When you feel complete, turn to your partner and talk together about what has taken place. Have your feelings and attitudes about your partner changed? Do you want to make some new choices about your interactions with your partner?

For a few minutes, simply commune silently with one another and see what happens. Allow any images, feelings, insights to emerge. . . .

Now take your leave of the Being(s), knowing that you can return at any time for more guidance and support. Return down the mountain to the meadow; move your awareness back into your body in the present moment, breathing, sensing, listening, until you are ready to open your eyes.

Make any additional notes you need about your experience.

∞

Over twenty years ago, in the early stages of our psychosynthesis training, my husband and I were guided on such an imaginary journey by our teachers at the time. I remember that I had a tendency to stride ahead up the trail, while my husband took more time to look around. I also recall how affirming the experience was for us, how it seemed that our relationship was blessed by the Being we met at the top (although I can no longer recall in what form the Being appeared).

Perhaps this is a way to reclaim the spiritual dimension of "marriage," using the word in its essential sense of long-term, committed personal partnership. Some people may hold their marriage within a spiritual context because of religious teachings. Many more, however, seem to have lost touch with this dimension through the stresses and demands of everyday life, and not much appears in our culture to remind us of this aspect. Paradoxically, when we remember to regard our most significant relationships within a context of larger purpose, the stresses and demands of daily life are more easily handled together.

CHILDREN AND FAMILY

Family systems theory and therapy are providing us with greater understanding than ever before of the complexities of family interactions and the difficulties of healthy family life. We have so much to learn after generations of parents' raising their children in the same ways they were raised without much questioning about the healthiness of these practices. There is a veritable explosion of books on family patterns and child rearing today; perhaps at long last we can learn to raise our children in love, rather than fear, helping them become the creative, confident adults we so sorely need in our troubled world.

Within the scope of this short chapter, I can add little to this rich field of ideas. I will limit our discussion here to a few pearls of wisdom about children and family that my husband and I learned from Dr. Assagioli and that we found invaluable in raising our two sons.

Imagine extending the idea of the Self of a couple to the family; imagine that each family has a Source of guidance and support that underlies the personalities of its members and the changing dynamics of the family system. Just as we can seek guidance from the Couple Self through meditation and imagery, we can seek the guidance of the Family Self.

Moreover, each child is a Self, underlying all his or her changing personality patterns and behaviors. Each child is striving to become the purest and strongest expression of Self in his or her unique way. Our job as parents is to nurture the developing personality so that its gifts can manifest themselves in the world. Our children are not in this world to meet our needs.

Honored Guests

Dr. Assagioli suggested that we regard our children as honored guests in our homes, here temporarily for the support and guidance we can give them to prepare for their journeys beyond our doors. I don't believe he meant that we should wait on our children as we might a guest; his analogy has more to do with an attitude of respect for and non-ownership of our children. They do not belong to us; they are only given into our care.

While we studied with Dr. Assagioli in 1973, our sons, aged four and seven, stayed with my husband's sister and her family. We knew they were in good hands, but when three weeks went by without our receiving any communication from home, I began to worry. I finally spoke to Dr. Assagioli about my concern. He suggested that I could turn over our sons to their Higher Selves. When I protested that it was only normal for a mother to worry, he replied, "Do you want to be just a normal mother?"

His suggestion and question challenged me to look beyond the cultural expectations of parenthood to a larger perspective. Our children are in fact always "under the care" of Self, as we all are. I could protect them from obvious dangers, and we had indeed provided responsibly for their care and protection while we were away. But ultimately, their fate was not and is not in my hands.

It may be hard for a "normal" parent to accept this fact, but when we do, we release both our children and ourselves from a terrible burden. Our children are freed to live their lives, go through their suffering, and find their paths without having to take care of our fears and demands. We as parents are freed from self-blame and constant anxiety about the way their lives unfold. Parents and children can become partners in life's adventure, increasingly supporting and loving each other as equals.

LARGER RELATIONSHIPS

And what of our relationship to our communities? To our nation? The planet? The Divine? Wholeness is about relationship, at all levels of our being. Just as our inner wholeness must embrace all aspects of ourselves—physical, emotional, mental, and spiritual—we are each an aspect of the greater Whole of community, nation, and humanity. For a community, nation, or the human family to grow whole, the rich diversity and complexity of its members must be embraced, included, accepted, integrated. How we relate to one another, then, affects the wholeness and health of our communities—local, national, and planetary.

And there is more; there is a larger Whole of the planet itself, the interdependent web of life of which humanity is only a part. We have relationships with the flora and fauna of our planet, sharing air, water, and land with them all. How we live affects the life support system we share in common with the flora and fauna, and of which they are such a vital part. When we cut down a rain forest, we lose the myriad species that live there, and we lose the oxygen-processing trees and plants that function as the lungs of the planet. Wind patterns and other dynamics of climate are affected worldwide.

When we sacrifice a spotted owl while clear-cutting old-growth redwoods in the Pacific Northwest, we lose more than a small shy bird seldom seen by humans. We lose an ecosystem that plays a vital and complex role in the health of the whole region. And we lose a source of great spiritual nourishment as we strip our world of beauty.

Considering the destructive effects of so much of our "civilized" ways, some people have come to regard humanity as a cancer growing on the planet. The analogy doesn't hold, however, because cancer doesn't usually have the capacity to serve its host (although some human hosts are able to use the experience as a teaching). Admittedly, we have not done much to benefit the planet up until now; indeed, even if humans suddenly disappeared from the face of the Earth, it is possible that we have so polluted and damaged the life-support systems of the planet that life would be severely compromised for eons to come. But we do have the capacity to heal and transform. We may now be essential to the healing of the wounds we have wrought.

We All Must Live in Relationship

Healing requires relationship. If we treat the ecosystem like an automobile engine, fixing this, adjusting that, we will only make things worse. We must live in relationship, allowing ourselves to be affected, instructed, changed, broken, and healed. If we are to bring our splendid human intelligence to the task at hand, we must come into relationship with the far greater Intelligence of nature.

We are put on this Earth in limited form to learn the things of the Heart through Touching. So be it. Let us allow ourselves to be touched in our relationships with every manifestation of life around us. Let us open our hearts to be touched by our friends, our partners, our children, the people of our communities, and human beings around the world. Let us open our hearts to be touched by birds, furry critters, elephants, and whales; by roses, weeds, and redwood trees; by sunsets, mountains, oceans, and clouds. We are all together in this life; we are all the stuff of Self.

12. Service: The Practice of Wholeness

> *We all have, without exception, a very deep longing to give—to give to the earth, to give to others, to give to the society, to work, to love, to care for this earth. That's true for every human being. And even the ones who don't find it, it's because it has been squashed or somehow suppressed in some brutal way in their life. But it's there to be discovered. We all long for that.*
>
> *And there's a tremendous sorrow for a human being who doesn't find a way to give. One of the worst of human sufferings is not to find a way to love, or a place to work and give of your heart and your being.[1]*
>
> —Jack Kornfield

WE BEGAN THIS JOURNEY TOGETHER with words of concern about the future of life on Earth. We asked, "How can we help awaken our human potential and put it to work to support peace, justice, and environmental harmony in the world?" We've held this question throughout our explorations, noting how our personal transformation and wholeness may affect the world around us. Now we'll focus more on the second part of the question and explore specifically how we can put our awakened potential "to work to support peace, justice, and environmental harmony in the world." In a word, let's talk about service.

Unfortunately, *service* has often been associated primarily with self-sacrifice, suffering, and, in latter-day terminology, codependence, or taking inappropriate responsibility for other people at one's own expense. I want to reclaim the word from these limiting associations because I am convinced that service is what we are really all about. Service is what happens when we act from our essential interrelatedness. Serving others counteracts the forces of separation, the greed and hatred that are destroying the very life-support systems of our planet. Serving others helps create a world of love and harmony in which we can all live more happily. Service is truly "enlightened self-interest."

Service comes naturally to us when we love and accept ourselves on a deep level. Our love bubbles up and overflows to those around us. We find our greatest satisfaction and fulfillment in making contributions to the world in ways that are uniquely our own. This is hardly self-sacrifice! It is the practice of wholeness.

WE ARE SET FREE

When we know ourselves to be, most essentially, spiritual beings—Self acting through particular personalities and organisms—we are set free from the fear of being "selfish," a fear that so often plagues the good children of our culture. When we plunge deeply into who we are, we discover we are creatures of great potential who yearn to use our potential to serve and participate in the living Being of Earth. We truly can trust ourselves. It is only when we identify with confused subpersonalities that we fall out of harmony. Then our true needs may become distorted into "selfish" desires and addictions, the pursuit of which can lead to harm for others and ourselves. As we discover Who we really are, our true needs and preferences lead us back into harmony. To be truly Self-centered is to be a giver of gifts to the world.

Our service is most satisfying and effective when it comes out of self-knowledge, matching our interests and talents. Self-knowledge also helps us be less confused about our motives and purpose, so we can move with greater clarity and respond in the moment to the ever-new opportunities that unfold before us. I hope that the ideas and exercises offered in this book have helped you move closer to knowing who you most deeply are, preparing you for richer service in our troubled world.

At the same time, doing service itself helps us grow whole. It challenges us to call upon talents and qualities we didn't know we had and bring them into play in our lives. It confronts us with fears, doubts, and outmoded beliefs, demanding that we work them through so that we can get on with the job at hand. So we don't need to wait until we have it all together to begin to serve; even if we think we have it all together, we will soon discover through serving just exactly where and how we do not!

Work on Yourself First

Still, I have waited for the last chapter to focus on service for good reason. You who have chosen to read and work with this book have from the first demonstrated your desire to serve; the book is written with that assumption clearly in mind. Sometimes it is hard for people who want to serve to take the time to work on themselves; they feel that it is a self-indulgent luxury they cannot afford in the face of the tremendous problems and suffering in our world. I wanted to invite you to step back from the fray for a while, to go inside, to give yourself the attention you need in order to serve from your deepest and truest nature. Such service is what the world truly needs.

FINDING THE PATH OF HEART

I believe one of the most precious gifts I received from Roberto Assagioli was his "permission" to let myself off the hook of taking care of everything wrong on the planet! When I studied with him in 1973, I told him how guilty I felt that I was not helping the people who were starving in Bangladesh. I tended at that time to take on emotionally every problem I heard about, whether or not I actually did anything concrete in response. Roberto looked at me with his loving gaze and said, "This is not your dharma. Other people are taking care of this problem. You have other work to do." *Dharma* is a Buddhist word meaning, among other things, a calling or spiritual duty.

I felt tremendous relief, because I felt in my heart that he had spoken the truth. His words helped me let go of my fearful and egotistic belief that somehow I was personally responsible for everything that was wrong on the planet (or at least everything I knew about). He reminded me that there are always other people working to serve, heal, and transform, and that I have my own path to follow, my own dharma. Don Juan, a Yaqui Indian shaman, calls it "the path of heart."[2]

In *Compassion in Action—Setting Out on the Path of Service,* Ram Dass outlines some criteria for deciding whether an act of service is appropriate to the moment. He suggests that we consider our values; our skills, talents, and personality characteristics; our opportunities; our existing responsibilities; and "the diverse roles we are called upon to fulfill in the moment."[3]

Ram Dass goes on to comment on the difficulty of taking all this into consideration for every act, and suggests that we need to rely on intuition a good deal of the time. I agree with that. Nevertheless, I think we can use these areas of concern as conscious guidelines for finding the path of heart.

Let's consider each of these in turn. First, is an act or area of service in keeping with our values? This might seem to go without saying, but I know that occasionally I am tempted to do something for someone that is in conflict with my values. I may think that this comes out of my desire to serve, but in fact, it may come out of a desire to please, to be liked, to belong. Allowing a friend to smoke in my vicinity is an example. I want to be nice, to accommodate my friend's preferences, but in doing so, I compromise my values regarding health and my own well-being.

What are our deepest values? They are not always easy to articulate, especially in the abstract. Our values make themselves known in relationship, in situations and challenges that life presents to us. Here's one way we can clarify our personal values in relation to the planetary challenges we all face together.

❦

Love and Anguish About the World

Have paper or your journal ready for writing. Then take a few minutes to bring your attention inside; pay quiet attention to your breathing, your sensations, feelings, and thoughts. . . .

You will be asking yourself two questions in turn. After each one, allow images, scenes, sensations, and whatever else to come. Allow your feelings to respond. Take plenty of time to contemplate each question, writing as you go along, or making notes when you feel finished.

> *1. What do I love most about life on Earth?*
> *2. What troubles me most about the world?*

When you are finished, look over what you have written. What are the values revealed here? What is really important to you? What areas of concern seem to call to you? Make some notes for future reference.

∞

We each have our own particular skills, talents, and personality characteristics to offer in our service. A path of heart is one that suits who one is, with one's unique set of interests, gifts, talents, skills, and characteristics. An introverted person with interest in meditation may not serve well as the organizer of a soup kitchen, no matter how valuable that form of service may be. This person may, on the other hand, be extremely effective in helping other people develop their own meditation practice, a service that a talented organizer might find quite difficult.

So, let's explore this further. What are your particular skills, interests, and personality characteristics? What are your special gifts? What are the qualities you most readily demonstrate in your life?

∞

Qualities, Gifts, and Service

Have ready your journal or other paper for writing. Take a few moments to breathe, relax your body, and bring your attention within.

When you are ready, begin looking back through your life, a few years at a time, and notice things you have done that you believed you did especially well and that you enjoyed doing. You may think of them as achievements, accomplishments, or simply high points. Make a list of these events, leaving plenty of space beneath each item for more notes. Try to include one or two events each from your childhood and adolescence, and at least three from your adult life. Don't limit yourself: the more the merrier!

Now review your list and note under each entry the positive impact it had on the world around you. How was that activity or accomplishment of service to others? If you don't think it was, look further!

Now note under each item what it was that you yourself *did,* exactly *how* you contributed to the venture. What were the skills you brought into play?

Note under each entry what your relationship to others seemed to be, what role you tended to take in the activity (team leader, team member, alone, doing my part separately from the others, coordinator, teacher, etc.). . . .

Next, note under each entry what it was about the activity or venture that gave you satisfaction. What was the "payoff" in your inner sense of satisfaction? Be as specific as possible. . . .

Looking back over your notes, see if you can see any patterns emerging: forms of service, patterns of skills or abilities, role or relationship with others, and feelings of satisfaction. See if you can identify six to eight primary skills. Can you find an essential role or relationship that seems to be at work throughout all the events? Do you find a similar source of satisfaction at the heart of each activity?

Now move into a more meditative state, relaxing your body, feelings, and thoughts. Imagine holding all you have discovered in a large bowl before you: the ways you have served, your skills, the role you tend to play, and what seems to be the essential source of satisfaction for you. Wait to see if any new insight comes to you about yourself and your gifts, and make some notes if you like. . . .

Now ask yourself what qualities you seem to have expressed in all of these activities, through these skills, in this role and relationship, and within this source of satisfaction. What qualities has Self sought to express through your endeavors?

Imagine bringing this quality or qualities into even fuller expression in your life right now. In what ways are you already doing this? In what new ways might you manifest these qualities even more richly? How will the quality or qualities help your service in the world? Visualize yourself in an activity expressing one of these qualities, noticing how others respond, what gets in the way, and how you move around and through these obstacles. . . .

If the spirit moves you, create a drawing to represent your qualities and gifts, and/or write an affirmation about them. You may want to simply sit for a while and experience these qualities within yourself. Give yourself plenty of time to integrate what you have learned and make any notes you need.[4]

Sometimes a process like this may bring up subpersonalities who either object to your acknowledging your gifts, or who try to take control of them. If so, it might be helpful to dialogue with whatever subpersonality is on the scene to find out about its needs and what it has to offer. You might also enjoy a consultation with your Wise Being.

Many of us need to have more appreciation for our gifts and qualities, for the special way each of us does things. We may have skills we have taken for granted that we might put to better use when we acknowledge their value. Remembering something we did as a child may help us discover skills, a role, or qualities that have been lying fallow ever since, ready now to be reawakened.

Many people discover that making use of their gifts and qualities is what gives them the greatest satisfaction and joy. This is a profound discovery. I wonder if so many people pursue material goods, money, power, and "fun" because they have never experienced the joy of true Self-expression. I believe the more we put our gifts to work in the world, the happier we will be.

Next, we might consider what opportunities are available to us to serve in our local community, at our place of work, among our circle of family and friends. We may not have to look far to find meaningful and appropriate tasks for ourselves, if we keep ourselves open to the unexpected.

Nevertheless, I have sometimes become quite anxious in the face of an opportunity. I fall into a belief that "opportunity knocks but once" and if I don't respond to it, I will lose out forever. Through experience, however, I have learned that quite the opposite is true. There are always numerous opportunities for service and Self-expression, all around me, all the time. All I need to do is move into silence and receptivity. Then I can more clearly hear both the knock of opportunity and the inner voice that guides me to respond. Mirabai Bush says it simply and elegantly: "We need to listen for what we know to be true, and do what we love to do."[5]

Sparks of Light

Jewish Hasidic masters teach of each person's responsibility to redeem the sparks of divine light that have become scattered and lost throughout the world, separated from God. We can redeem these sparks by recognizing the divine spark within everything and everyone we encounter and through acts of loving kindness and healing. But no one of us can redeem all the sparks. Each of us can redeem only those sparks that "fit" our own soul, our own spiritual physiognomy or "soul root." We are like finely tuned receivers, aware of energy flow only at certain frequencies; these are the particular sparks for us to redeem.[6]

What opportunities for service call to you each day? Try keeping a daily log of these opportunities for a while in your journal. Just notice them, without expecting yourself to respond to any or all of them. In time, it may become more obvious what opportunities call especially to you, which ones fit your soul root.

First Responsibilities First

And what about our existing responsibilities? A parent of small children has responsibilities to them first. No matter how noble the cause, neglecting one's children creates more suffering in the world, not less. Our service must begin with our existing responsibilities to family and friends, and then move out from there.

On the other hand, we can load ourselves up with apparent "responsibilities" that allow no time or energy for fulfilling service. "I'd like to help, but . . . I have to put in overtime at work again this week," or "I have four committee meetings to attend already." We may need to extricate ourselves from nonessential and socially defined responsibilities to make space for more satisfying activities along our path of service.

Finally, does an act or area of service honor the diverse roles we are called upon to fulfill in the moment? When I am responsible for leading a workshop or meeting, it doesn't make sense for me to spend time cleaning the bathrooms at the conference center. It isn't that the work is beneath me; it is simply that I have another role to fulfill and my first responsibility must be to doing that one well. On the other hand, if my chosen role is to be a support person, it might be more appropriate for me to clean the bathrooms than to try to plan the daily schedule of events.

Jimmy and Rosalynn Carter had definite roles to fulfill when he served as President of the United States. Later, when they left the White House, they took on roles as volunteer construction workers, helping Habitat for Humanity build homes for the poor in Uganda and on the Lower East Side of Manhattan. Each set of roles was significant, but they could not be fulfilled at the same time.

Taking these areas of concern into account may help us to discover appropriate forms of service for ourselves. By considering our values, our skills and talents, our opportunities, our existing responsibilities, and the various roles we are called to fulfill, we take stock of ourselves and our situations, seeking forms of service that express who and where we are, right now. Then the path we choose is more likely to be a path of heart.

FORMS OF SERVICE AND SELF-EXPRESSION

What forms might our service to the world take? Can we serve only by feeding hungry people, building housing for the homeless, or caring for the sick and dying? These forms are powerful and can teach us much about suffering, our own and others', our fears and avoidances. Yet these are not the only ways we can express Self in service to the world. We also serve by creating beauty through art, music, and dance.

We serve by creating useful tools, supportive environments, shelter, order, and safety. We serve through teaching, counseling, guiding, healing, and inspiring. We serve by bringing laughter, emotional release, and simple pleasure to others. We serve by facilitating the exchange of information.

We serve others as parents, supportive family members, and friends. We serve by making connections between people, and between people and the natural environment. We serve by protecting and restoring the natural environment. We serve by seeking new understanding through research and philosophical inquiry, and sharing our insights with others.

A Brain-Wave Experiment

We also serve by simply showing up. Our presence in a situation can be healing all by itself, without our consciously doing anything. This has been demonstrated in many studies. One experimenter measured the brain-wave synchronization of people placed together in a room.[7] Brain-wave synchronization means that the two hemispheres of the brain are producing similar wavelengths at the same time and in the same phase; this is associated with peacefulness, clarity, and overall well-being.

It was discovered that a person with unsynchronized brain waves became more synchronized when in the presence of someone with highly synchronized brain waves, without any overt communication taking place between them. It was also found that the highly synchronized subject lost some ground, but not nearly as much as the other person gained. The implications are that we truly can spread peace and joy simply by being peaceful and joyful ourselves.

RIGHT LIVELIHOOD

Sometimes our livelihood is our major form of service, following Buddha's precept regarding "right livelihood." We are fortunate if this is so. We may still seek other forms of service outside our regular paid employment, however, to give expression to other sides of ourselves, and to experience the joy of giving without any expectation of return.

For some, it becomes difficult to distinguish between paid work and volunteer activities because one seems to flow into the other. For others, it is important to have two different forms of expression. One person who works as an accountant might want to help low-income people with their tax returns, while another, similarly employed, would prefer to volunteer as a basketball coach at a local youth center.

As you examine your potential forms of service, begin with what you do now, with your work, your family responsibilities, your hobbies and volunteer activities. Affirm what you are already doing before asking if you need to do more. Chances are that you are already serving the world in myriad ways, moving simply and without fanfare out of your natural inclinations and out of your own growing wholeness.

If there seems to be room for more or an impulse to try something different, then pull out the stops. Seek within to discover what it is that wants to emerge, what quality, skill, or capacity is asking for expression. Look around your community and locality to discover what calls forth your interest and creativity. It is when who-we-are meets what-is-needed that we find our best forms of service.

I'M GREAT! NO BIG DEAL.

In order to really be of service, we need to acknowledge our gifts—how else can we put them to work? But for many of us, such acknowledgment is threatening; we are afraid of becoming arrogant. We have been taught to be modest and unassuming. This may be more of a problem for women than for men in our society; I am not sure. I believe, however, that it constitutes a major barrier to service for many people.

Modesty is a valuable quality in its own right; it is closely related to humility, which keeps us connected to the Earth and with those around us, reminding us of how much we still have to learn. Service without humility could be officious, intrusive, even degrading to the other person.

Acknowledging Our Gifts

I believe, however, that humility can and should include acknowledgment of our gifts, our "greatness." Otherwise, it is an inferiority complex in disguise. We can humbly accept the gifts we have been given, develop them, and put them to use in the world. This may mean "going public" with them, being willing to say, "I'm quite skilled in that area. I can take on that job." It's like simply acknowledging that we are a certain height, that we have a certain color of eyes or hair. It is allowing our greatness to pass through us and out into the world.

The fear of standing out in the crowd can keep us in denial about our own greatness, even within the privacy of our own mind. It's as if the biblical teaching "Do not let your left hand know what your right hand is doing" applies to our self-image, as well as to the giving of alms. For many years, I limited my effectiveness as a teacher and counselor in this way, afraid of holding too high an opinion of myself. I tried to hide my light under a bushel basket, another thing the Bible advises us not to do! It was the persistent feedback and encouragement of many friends that helped me to accept responsibility for my talents and take the risk of making them more visible to the world.

Each of us is great, in our own way. And it's no big deal. We needn't fear being who we are, only trying to be who we are not. Generally speaking, we are much greater than we have been led to believe. And we are responsible for developing and acting on our greatness, for the sake of the world.

∽

Acknowledge Your Gifts

Take a few minutes to acknowledge your special qualities and gifts, some of which you may have explored earlier in this book. Notice in what ways you are great. What happens when you try to acknowledge this to yourself? What inner voices of denial and doubt speak up?

Is there a way you can verbally affirm your talents and greatness to yourself, a way that is humble and realistic and that takes responsibility for your gifts? For example, you might try saying, *I have the gift of ___ and I am committed to putting this gift into service in the world,* or *I am a talented ___ and I'm willing to serve in this way.* (Don't worry if this sounds corny; no one else needs to hear it, and besides, it's for a good cause.)

∽

MEETING THE NEEDS OF THE SERVER

Probably most of the problems that sabotage our service stem from our tendency to ignore and neglect our own needs. It is so easy to suppress our needs in favor of an important cause; we feel so noble and get such strokes from others. But it is dangerous to do so, because our unmet needs will act on us on an unconscious level, leading to burnout, power struggles, or attempts to help others in completely inappropriate ways.

Sometimes We Must Sacrifice

There are times when we must set aside our personal comfort and desires for a while in order to respond to an emergency or accommodate ourselves to a difficult situation. Sometimes service does demand sacrifice. It is one thing, however, to make a conscious choice in such a situation, and another thing altogether to pretend to oneself and others that one simply has no such needs.

We are not always going to get our needs met. We may have to keep going without sufficient rest or food, without support and appreciation from others, or without any indications of success. If we insist on getting our needs met first, we may never undertake any service at all. The challenge is to remain aware of our needs, monitor them, find ways to meet them as much as we can, and keep the love flowing within ourselves for the parts that feel overwhelmed. As in all relationships, we are the only ones who can take responsibility for our feelings and needs, and we must, in order to serve.

Let me share a personal example. One way I work out my own inner conflicts is by talking with someone who is a good listener. So when I led a group of psychosynthesis trainers on a citizen diplomacy exchange in the former Soviet Union, I made sure we had frequent meetings to talk about what was going on for us. Most of the time this worked well, because other members of the group had similar needs. Sometimes it didn't, however, because as leader of the group, I would be so busy trying to facilitate the meeting that I wouldn't have an adequate opportunity to talk about my own concerns. I would try to bring them out through other people, instead of owning them myself. This led to confusion and tension in the group.

Finally, by talking with one of the group members privately, I was able to see how I was projecting my own needs and issues onto the group, sometimes inappropriately. I realized afterward that I would do better to ask someone to help me work through my own concerns, probably without involving the whole group. Asking for help might be hard for me to do, because I tend to devalue my own needs unless they are reflected in the common needs of the others.

Good Intentions

I know I am not alone in this tendency to project my own, often unconscious, needs onto those I am attempting to serve. I have seen the dreary little missions along the highway in northern New Mexico, missions supported by good, caring Christians who sincerely wanted to help the Indians, missions that succeeded primarily in subverting the tribal structure and the harmonious way of life of the Navajo peoples. I imagine that the early missionaries compared the Navajo ways of life with their own, decided what they themselves would need (and did need) in such a situation, and proceeded to impose that willy-nilly on the Navajo. This is an extreme example, perhaps, but it vividly demonstrates how we must listen to and consult with those whom we would serve, and vigilantly keep our own needs to ourselves.

Burnout

Another common result of suppressing our personal needs is burnout; we use up our energies in the midst of the fray, and if we don't replenish ourselves, we finally run dry. Often we hold out the promise to ourselves of a successful outcome for our endeavors, an outcome that will make it all worthwhile. When that outcome fails to materialize, we feel betrayed, angry, hopeless. We have sacrificed ourselves, and for what? We may become disillusioned, even cynical and bitter.

Go with the Flow

Letting go of results is one of the hardest things to do in any endeavor in life. Of course we want a positive outcome. Of course we want to succeed in reducing suffering, transforming consciousness, saving the world. Letting go of results doesn't mean we cease to care about what happens. It only means we find our primary satisfaction in the doing itself.

In practicing hatha yoga, for example, one can focus on trying to do the poses perfectly, comparing oneself constantly to others in the class or pictures in a book. Especially as a beginner, one would experience a lot of frustration and self-doubt, and might give up altogether. Or one could focus on the sensations of stretching and release in the muscles while doing the poses, and consequently would feel energized and satisfied each time one practices.

When we let go of results and enjoy the doing, we feel whole and complete, no matter what the vicissitudes of fate. We take care of ourselves as we go along and avoid deferring to an anticipated end that may never come.

Letting go of results frees our actions to take us in unexpected directions. We may begin with one goal in mind and find ourselves succeeding in another way we never considered. A group of citizens attempting to prevent freeway construction through a delicate ecosystem might not succeed in stopping the freeway, but their efforts might raise public awareness sufficiently to prevent other environmental abuses in the area. If the group members allowed the freeway defeat to discourage them, they would be less able to direct this aroused awareness toward the other problems.

To find our satisfaction in the deeds themselves, we work from a base of self-knowledge and wholeness. We take care of our essential needs for belonging, support, and appreciation. We work in an area that calls upon our gifts and offers us the challenge of learning new skills. Then we feel fulfilled even when we fall short of our goals or cannot determine the effects of what we have done.

A CHALLENGING FIELD

Counseling is a field that constantly challenges the practitioner to let go of results. When working with an individual, a counselor often has no idea of where this person will go, or how he or she will develop. Sessions unfold mysteriously, full of surprises and full of stuck places where nothing seems to move for long periods of time. If counselors become attached to a "cure," to seeing the person changed in any particular way, they are doomed to stress and burnout. They will also probably create unproductive conflict with their clients who will struggle, and rightly so, to do things in their own way and time.

Usually counselors who become attached to outcome are attempting to get their own needs met, needs to feel good about themselves and their work. They are saying, in effect, "Get better in such-and-such a way so that I can prove what a good therapist I am." Of course, counselors, like anyone else, have a legitimate need to feel competent in their work, but that sense of competence must come out of the totality of their work, not from a particular client during a particular period of time.

AVOIDING SHOULDS AND OUGHTS

Our motives, and therefore our actions, may also be undermined by old programming about "What We Should Be Doing" or "How We Ought to Serve." Rather than acting out of our innate abilities and according to the demands of the situation, we look for a rule book outside ourselves to tell us what we're supposed to do. Our needs for approval can muddle our clarity of purpose. We pay close attention to the opinions of those around us, especially authority figures, trying to pick up clues from them about what we should be doing. In the process, we fail to listen to our own inner guidance. We may even fail to notice what is really going on with those around us, because we are so focused on their judgements about us.

When I am driven by "shoulds" and "oughts," I am focused on my needs, not on the needs of the other person, or of the larger Whole. There is a kind of tension in my service arising out of my hidden agenda to "do right." My service may still be helpful to others; in fact, much useful service is probably done from this motivation. But I believe I am both happier and more effective when I act primarily from my inner sense of rightness, whether or not that agrees with others' expectations.

Doing the Right Thing

Sometimes I find it helpful to remind myself that everyone around me is probably also worrying about what other people think (including me), and whether or not they are "doing the right thing." There are no ultimate human authorities about any choice in life; we are all just muddling along as best we can, moment to moment, day to day. No one knows more about my life situation than I do, so no one knows better than I what I should be doing in the way of service. There is no rule book in the sky. Even sacred writings like those in the Bible are open to interpretation. So all I can do at any moment is act on the basis of my own best judgement, which integrates perspectives and information gleaned from others as well as a lot of inner work.

As you go about your service work, in whatever form it takes, notice any inner voice that nags at you, giving you directions that include words like "should." If you can, take a few minutes to consider when and where you may have acquired that voice. What seems to be its motive in your life? Does it reflect the realities of your life now? If it is a particularly persistent inner voice, you might explore it as a subpersonality, seeking to appreciate its wants, its true needs, and what truth and quality it might have to offer you. In this way, even the intrusive "should" can become a partner in your Self expression and service.

Ongoing Growth

Ongoing service calls for ongoing growth on our part as we continue to uncover old wounds and old programming that block our free-flowing expression of Self. The paradox is that we can and do manage to be of service to our world, no matter how wounded and blocked we are. Our impulse to reach out, connect, and make a difference in the world is simply too strong to be suppressed. And as we act on that impulse, no matter how imperfectly, we grow into wholeness ourselves, together with those we serve.

Meeting our needs often means giving ourselves the opportunity to renew ourselves, alone and with others' help. The brain-wave study cited earlier demonstrates how important it is for us to do this, for although those with synchronized brain waves had a beneficial effect on others, they would begin to lose ground after a time. Being around people who are frightened and confused can gradually pull us into similar states of mind. We may need in turn to seek the company of others who manifest peace and joyfulness. We may need to allow others to take over our tasks for a while, so we can meditate, pray, commune with nature, or simply play.

Accepting Gifts from Others

Just as we are called to serve others, others are called to serve us. Sometimes it is a greater challenge to accept another's love and assistance than it is to offer our own service. I recall a piece of wisdom that my father once shared with me, something he in turn had learned from his father. Accepting another's gift is giving a gift to the giver, for we are allowing the other person the pleasure of the giving. I would add to this thought that there may be situations when we are unable to accept the gift itself, but we can always accept with gratitude the generous impulse beneath it.

When we see ourselves as interconnected parts of a larger Whole, it becomes clear that there is really no distinction between serving and being served. We are always recipients of and participants in the ongoing exchange of energy that is life. When I bathe the forehead of a sick child, I receive as much as I give, for I am enriched by the connection and love the child and I share. Every gift we give freely, out of the fullness of our hearts, comes back to us in numerous ways. Every gift we accept with gratitude and humility enriches us and the giver, together.

Service is the practice of wholeness; it is wholeness happening. This is true no matter which role we play in the exchange. Service is at the heart of spiritual practice in every religion. It is the most satisfying and fulfilling way of life. Yet somehow, many of us in the industrialized world have largely forgotten this wisdom, seeking instead the short-term thrill of material acquisition and power over others. Our life-support systems are dying as a result.

Now it is time for us to reaffirm our interconnectedness with all of life on Earth, and to recommit ourselves to living lives of wholeness, community, and service.

The dedication from the United Nations Environmental Sabbath program on the next page says it well.[8]

We join with the earth and with each other
To bring new life to the land.
To restore the waters.
To refresh the air.

We join with the earth and with each other
To renew the forests
To care for the plants
To protect the creatures.

We join with the earth and with each other
To celebrate the seas
To rejoice in the sunlight
To sing the song of the stars.

We join with the earth and with each other
To recreate the human community
To promote justice and peace
To remember our children.

We join with the earth and with each other.
We join together as many and diverse expressions of one
    loving mystery:
 for the healing of the earth and the renewal of all life.

Thank you for joining me on this journey toward wholeness
for us all.

Notes

CHAPTER 1
SELF-AWARENESS: THE FIRST STEP

1. I first experienced this exercise as led by Harry Sloan at the former Psychosynthesis Institute in San Francisco, but I do not know if he was the creator of the process.

2. Charlotte Joko Beck, *Everyday Zen* (San Francisco: HarperCollins, 1989), 51.

3. The process as described is adapted from an exercise by James and Susan Vargiu, training handout, 1971.

CHAPTER 2
BEGINNING WHERE WE ARE NOW

1. Ira Progoff, *At a Journal Workshop* (New York: Dialogue House, 1975).

2. John G. Neihardt, *Black Elk Speaks* (Lincoln: University of Nebraska Press, 1961).

3. Piero Ferrucci, *What We May Be* (Los Angeles: Tarcher, 1982), 115.

4. Ibid.

5. Charlotte Joko Beck, *Everyday Zen,* 29.

CHAPTER 3
STRENGTHENING OUR CENTER

1. Roberto Assagioli in an interview with Sam Keen, "The Golden Mean of Roberto Assagioli," *Psychology Today,* December 1974.

2. Joanna Macy, *World as Lover, World as Self* (Berkeley: Parallax, 1991), 12.

3. The source of this technique is Roberto Assagioli, personal instruction, 1973.

4. Ram Dass, *Journey of Awakening* (New York: Bantam, 1978).

CHAPTER 4
WHAT'S POSSIBLE?

1. In Assagioli's original diagram, there is a radiating point or star at the top, representing Self and placed there to indicate Self's direct energizing of the superconscious and contact with both the individual and the universal. A dotted line connects the radiating star with the "I" point in the center to indicate that the "I" is a reflection of Self. However, Thomas Yeomans, a psychosynthesis theorist, has proposed that depicting Self in this way is too limiting. It may create the impression that Self is closer to the superconscious and removed from the basic unconscious. It might encourage us to scorn our bodies in favor of our intellects, or to separate ourselves from nature. Yeomans has proposed the version used here, with no point or star for Self. Self underlies and permeates all dimensions of the conscious and unconscious, the individual and the collective, beyond our ability to draw it into a diagram.

2. This exercise synthesizes ideas and techniques from many sources.

CHAPTER 5
SETTING OUR SIGHTS

1. Dr. Martin Luther King, Jr., "I Have a Dream" delivered at the March on Washington, August 28, 1963, qtd. in *Read, Reason, Write* by Dorothy U. Seyler (New York: Random House, 1987).

2. This exercise synthesizes ideas and techniques from many sources.

3. This exercise was developed by the author and Walter Polt of Intermountain Associates for Psychosynthesis in New Mexico.

4. James Thurber's well-known story, *The Secret Life of Walter Mitty,* has appeared in numerous anthologies.

5. This exercise is adapted from one developed by the former Psychosynthesis Institute, Redwood City, California, and based upon Roberto Assagioli's exercise in *Psychosynthesis* (New York: Penguin, 1976), 166-67.

CHAPTER 6
WORKING WITH BLOCKS IN OUR PATH

1. Like the others in the series, this exercise is a synthesis of ideas and techniques from many sources.

2. This exercise is a synthesis of ideas and techniques from many sources.

CHAPTER 7
TRANSFORMING THE DEMONS WITHIN

1. This exercise is based on one designed by Vivian King.

2. This process is offered through "Despair and Empowerment" workshops and described by Joanna Macy in *Despair and Personal Power in the Nuclear Age* (Philadelphia: New Society, 1983).

3. The term "toxic shame" comes from John Bradshaw, *Healing the Shame that Binds You* (Deerfield Beach: Health Communications, 1988).

CHAPTER 8
LIVING WILL FULLY

1. Roberto Assagioli, *The Act of Will* (New York: Penguin, 1974), 47.
2. Ibid.

3. Ibid.
4. Ibid., 86-87.

CHAPTER 9
CHOOSING TO CHANGE

1. Roberto Assagioli, *The Act of Will,* 86-87.

CHAPTER 10
WHAT TO DO WHEN WE SEE THE LIGHT

1. Annie Dillard, *Holy the Firm* (New York: HarperCollins, 1977).

2. Rev. Dan O'Neal, sermon, Santa Rosa, California, November 1991.

3. Vaclav Havel, *Disturbing the Peace* (New York: HarperCollins, 1990), 10-12.

4. Thich Nhat Hanh, *The Miracle of Mindfulness* (Boston: Beacon, 1975).

5. This version was composed by Morgan Farley of Santa Fe, New Mexico, for a 1980 workshop.

6. Frank Haronian, "The Repression of the Sublime," Monograph, Psychosynthesis Research Foundation, 1967.

7. John Firman, in a lecture at Psychosynthesis Institute, Summer 1977.

8. I am grateful to Tom Yeomans for making this distinction. See "The Three Dimensions of Psychosynthesis," *Readings in Psychosynthesis,* vol. 2 (Toronto: The Ontario Institute for Studies in Education, 1988), 243.

9. Roberto Assagioli, *Psychosynthesis,* 6-7.

10. From *Plum Village Chanting Book* (Berkeley: Parallax Press, 1991), 131, a collection of chants, prayers, and meditations used at Plum Village in France; Thich Nhat Hanh is the spiritual leader of this Vietnamese Buddhist refuge.

CHAPTER 11
RELATIONSHIPS: GROWING WHOLE TOGETHER

1. Hyemeyohsts Storm, *Seven Arrows* (New York: Ballantine, 1972).

2. Joanna Macy, *World as Lover, World as Self,* 160.

3. Piero Ferrucci, *What We May Be,* 175.

4. Ibid., 176.

5. Joanna Macy, *World as Lover, World as Self.*

6. To explore further the perspective of "mutual causality" and "dependent co-arising." I recommend Joanna Macy's book, *World as Lover, World as Self,* especially her discussion of the Buddhist principle of karma. Her subsequent book, *Mutual Causality in Buddhism and General Systems Theory,* offers a more scholarly and thorough presentation of these concepts.

7. Personal communication with Roberto Assagioli, summer 1973.

CHAPTER 12
SERVICE: THE PRACTICE OF WHOLENESS

1. Jack Kornfield in audiotape series, *Roots of Buddhist Psychology,* Dharma Seed Tape Library.

2. Carlos Casteneda, *The Teachings of Don Juan* (Berkeley: University of California, 1968).

3. Ram Dass and Mirabai Bush, *Compassion in Action* (New York: Bell Tower, 1992), 136.

4. Ideas for this exercise come from Arthur Miller's "System for Identifying Motivated Abilities," from Bolles and Crystal, *What Color Is Your Parachute?* 1981, and from an exercise by Tom Yeomans in a 1978 workshop in San Francisco.

5. Ram Dass and Mirabai Bush, *Compassion in Action,* 159.

6. This idea is discussed by Rabbi Art Green in *Seek My Face, Speak My Name* (Northvale, N.J.: Aronson, 1992), 188.

7. The experiment is described in Jacobo Grinber-Zylberbaum, *Creation of Experience,* Instituto Nacional para el Estudio de la Concienca, Mexico, 1988.

8. From Elizabeth Roberts and Elias Amidon, eds. *Earth Prayers* (San Francisco: HarperCollins, 1991), 94.

Glossary

Terms are defined here as they are specially used in psychosynthesis. Words common to other psychological approaches are not included unless they have a special meaning in psychosynthesis.

ATTACHMENT. A desire to acquire and/or keep something perceived as external to one's essential being, be it object, role, identity, relationship, or circumstances.

AWARENESS. The most basic experience of consciousness. It includes, but is not dependent on, perception, comprehension, analysis, and understanding. Awareness is considered to exist even without sensory input; it is the apprehension of being.

BALANCE. To bring parts of oneself into equal awareness and value so that each is used without any being in control.

CENTER. As in a wheel, the hub of power and balance; the personal experience of being unattached to and dis-identified from a particular object, event, or personality aspect.

CHOICE. Conscious or unconscious selection of attitude or action; the essential act of will.

CONTENT. The specific ideas, words, situations, feelings, sensations, and images contained in awareness.

COUPLE SELF. A source of purpose and energy for a couple; the hypothetical union of the Selves of the two partners.

DISIDENTIFICATION. The process of expanding one's sense of identity from being limited by a role, attitude, subpersonality, or other partial aspect of oneself.

DYNAMICS. The forces which produce motion and change in a system or process.

EMERGING. Coming into manifestation from the unconscious.

EMOTIONALLY IDENTIFIED. Perceiving oneself primarily in terms of one's feelings.

GROWTH. Development to a more inclusive, integrated, and effective whole person.

GUIDED IMAGERY. The use of symbols and imaginary situations to explore feelings and life patterns, either briefly or at length. May include visual, auditory, tactile, and kinesthetic imagery.

HIGHER SELF. A deep and all-inclusive center of identity and being within each person where individuality and universality blend. Also called simply "Self."

HIGHER UNCONSCIOUS. The realm of the unconscious from which originate more highly evolved impulses: altruistic love and will, humanitarian action, artistic and scientific inspiration, philosophic and spiritual insight, and the drive for purpose and meaning in life. Also called the superconscious.

"I." Traditionally, a synonym for the personal self, "I" refers to a sense of unchanging identity beneath transitory feelings, thoughts, and physical actions.

IDENTIFICATION (WITH). The act or process of including an experience or quality in one's sense of who one is. This can be a re-owning of a previously denied part of oneself, or it can be a limiting self-definition that excludes a larger reality. One can also identify with self.

IDENTITY. Self-concept; who one thinks and feels one is.

INNER DIALOGUE. A conversation between various symbols, figures, or voices within one's imagination.

INNER WISDOM. The deep knowledge and integrative faculty of the superconscious; although usually unconscious, it can be reached through meditation and other techniques.

INTENTION. Energetic willingness to move towards a purpose.

INTUITION. A holistic, synthetic apprehension of truth without reasoning or outer experience. Intuitive knowledge is in harmony with universal principles and originates in the superconscious.

KNOWING. Besides the traditional meaning, "knowing" can also refer to inner conviction, similar to inner wisdom and intuition.

LOVE. Used here in the sense of impersonal, altruistic love, which appreciates and desires to serve the highest and best in other people.

LOWER UNCONSCIOUS. The realm of the unconscious from which originate biological drives and instincts, and which is the repository for repressed past experiences.

MANIFEST. To bring into conscious, visible expression a pattern which heretofore has been unconscious and latent.

MEDITATION. Quiet, inward awareness used in many forms for the purpose of reaching a relatively pure experience of self and opening to superconscious patterns and techniques.

MENTALLY IDENTIFIED. Perceiving oneself primarily in terms of thoughts and intellectual capabilities.

MIND. In psychosynthesis, "mind" usually refers to the faculty of reasoning and other intellectual activities.

MODEL. An intellectual construct useful for presenting a concept which helps the mind to comprehend something indirectly, but which should not be mistaken for reality itself.

NEXT STEP. The new, larger whole towards which the natural process of growth is leading; implies a conscious choice to embrace and integrate this new pattern in one's daily life.

PATTERN. A constellation of interrelated energies. On the personality level, a pattern may manifest itself as behaviors, feelings, thoughts, intuition, and/or physical states.

PEAK EXPERIENCE. Periods of intensified perception, heightened emotion of an esctatic, pleasurable quality, and increased mental receptivity and apprehension, often including a sense of union and harmony with all Being—with one's highest conception of God.

PERSONAL PSYCHOSYNTHESIS. The process of growth leading to the integration of the personality around the personal self, a center of awareness and will.

PRESENCE. A quality of being focused, attentive, and fully aware of oneself and others, in the moment and on all levels—physical, emotional, mental, spiritual.

PROCESS. The totality of interactions and changing relationships between the various psychological and physiological energies of an individual or a group.

PROJECTION. The attributing of one's internal characteristics or conflicts onto external people, objects, or events.

PSYCHOSYNTHESIS. The natural growth process of human beings towards coherence, wholeness, and harmony, on the level of the personality and the individual as well as within relationships, groups, communities, and the whole of humanity.

PURPOSE. Motivating force or direction, underlying choice and action. Differs from a goal in that purpose is more fluid and abstract and can be fulfilled in numerous ways.

QUALITY. Usually, a transpersonal quality; attributes of character which reflect universal principles, such as love, strength, clarity, or harmony.

REACTIVE. Unconscious, automatic response to a stimulus, as opposed to a consciously chosen response.

RESISTANCE. Energy opposing the bringing of something to consciousness or expression; also, behavior having this effect.

RESPONSIBILITY. The conscious recognition and acceptance of one's capacity to choose the various aspects of one's life.

SELF. The source of individual awareness and will of which the personal self is a partial reflection; one's deepest and most essential identity which unites the individual with universal Being.

SELF. The personal self, the center of awareness and will which directs and harmonizes the personality; a reflection of Self.

SELF-EXPRESSION. The bringing into form through the personality of qualities and patterns originating from the Self.

SELF-REALIZATION. Awakening to one's true nature as Self and the expression of Self in one's life.

SERVICE. Activities which contribute to the growth and expansion of life; for each individual, service may take a specific form, such as humanitarian activities, teaching, healing, artistic or musical expression, ecological enhancement, etc.

SPIRITUAL. Pertaining to the realm of human experience and involving values, meaning, purpose, and the unification with universal principles, patterns, and energies.

SPIRITUAL PSYCHOSYNTHESIS. The alignment of the personal self and the personality with Self through a gradual assimilation of superconscious energies and their integration of the personality; a natural process which can be enhanced by conscious choice.

SUBPERSONALITY. A semi-autonomous "structured constellation of attitudes, drives, habit patterns, logical elements which is organized in adaptation to forces in the internal and external environment."—Martha Crampton, *Psychosynthesis: Some Key Aspects of Theory and Practice* (Montreal: Canadian Institute of Psychosynthesis, 1977).

SUPERCONSCIOUS. The higher unconscious.

SYNTHESIS. The transformation into a larger, inclusive whole of two or more previously disparate or conflicting elements.

TRANSCEND. To rise above, to raise one's consciousness and choice above the control of forces at a lower level.

TRANSFORMATION. An holistic, overall change in nature or form to one that is more inclusive and responsive to the needs of the present.

TRANSPERSONAL. Pertaining to experience which transcends or goes beyond personal, individual identity and meaning; involves values, meaning, purpose, and unification with universal principles; synonomous with spiritual.

TRANSPERSONAL SELF. Self or Higher Self; the source of individual identity and will which unites with the universal.

TRANSPERSONAL WILL. The will of Self; a unifying, synergistic force which brings the individual's life into harmony with universal principles.

UNIVERSAL BEING. The totality of essential Reality.

UNIVERSAL WILL. The essential intentionality expressed in all movement and relationship in the universe.

VISION. An ideal image of purpose and direction to be brought into manifestation in one's life.

WILL. The primary psychological function of the self through which every aspect of one's life is chosen and integrated; the capacity to choose and direct one's actions and destiny.

Bibliography

In addition to books cited in the text, I am including a few on psychosynthesis (starred ★) and some others which have been useful to me in developing my understanding and writing this book.

★Assagioli, Roberto. *Psychosynthesis.* New York: Penguin, 1976.

★Assagioli, Roberto. *The Act of Will.* New York: Penguin, 1974.

Beck, Charlotte Joko. *Everyday Zen.* San Francisco: HarperCollins, 1989.

★Brown, Molly Young. *The Unfolding Self: Psychosynthesis and Counseling.* Los Angeles: Psychosynthesis Press, 1983.

Dillard, Annie. *Holy the Firm.* New York: HarperCollins, 1977.

★Ferrucci, Piero. *What We May Be.* Los Angeles: Tarcher, 1982.

Hanh, T. N. *The Miracle of Mindfulness.* Boston: Beacon, 1975.

Havel, V. *Disturbing the Peace.* New York: HarperCollins, 1990.

Macy, Joanna. *Despair and Personal Power in the Nuclear Age.* Philadelphia: New Society, 1983.

Macy, Joanna. *World as Lover, World as Self.* Berkeley: Parallax, 1991.

Neihardt, John G. *Black Elk Speaks*. Lincoln: University of Nebraska Press, 1961.

Progoff, Ira. *At a Journal Workshop*. New York: Dialogue House, 1975.

★Rainwater, Janette. *You're In Charge!* Los Angeles: Guild of Tutors, 1979.

Ram Dass. *Journey of Awakening*. New York: Bantam, 1978.

Ram Dass, and Mirabai Bush. *Compassion in Action*. New York: Bell Tower, 1992.

Roberts, Elizabeth, and Elias Amidon, eds. *Earth Prayers*. San Francisco: HarperCollins, 1991.

★Sliker, Gretchen. *Multiple Mind: Healing the Split in Psyche and World*. Boston: Shambhala, 1992.

Small, Jacquelyn. *Awakening in Time: The Journey from Codependence to Co-Creation*. New York: Bantam, 1991.

★Stauffer, Edith. *Unconditional Love and Forgiveness*. Burbank: Triangle, 1987.

Storm, Hyemeyohsts. *Seven Arrows*. New York: Ballantine, 1972.

Taylor, Jeremy. *Dream work: Techniques for Discovering the Creative Power in Dreams*. Mahwah, N.J.: Paulist Press, 1983.

Taylor, Jeremy. *Where People Fly and Water Runs Uphill: Using Dreams to Tap the Wisdom of the Unconscious*. New York: Warner Books, 1992.

Index

More titles to support personal transformation...

Growing Whole
Exploring the Wilderness Within
An Audio and Guided Journal for Discovering Your Strengths, Creativity, and Wisdom
  by Molly Young Brown
  128 pp. journal and 60-min. cassette
  Practice the skills Molly Brown introduced you to in *Growing Whole* with this journal and audio set. Topics focused on in short essays, exercises, and guided experiences include self-awareness, strengthening your center, working with the blocks in your path to personal development, and more.
128 pp. journal and 60-min. cassette   Order No. 8329

Trusting Intuition
  by Helene Lerner-Robbins
  Trust yourself. You can have faith in your personal and spiritual progress. These innovative meditation books bolster your self-confidence and affirm that you are where you need to be in your journey of self-discovery.

  My Timing Is Always Right
    There are no coincidences and no mistakes. You are in the right place. Overcome worry and anxiety about the frustrations of daily situations. Discover the principle of syndronicity and why people, places, and things are as they should be—right now—in your life.
    96 pp.   Order No. 5471
  Embrace Change
    When old ways no longer work and new behaviors still feel uncomfortable, *Embrace Change*. These affirmations and meditations help you make the most of the day and focus on continuing personal growth. Find renewed courage for making changes in your attitudes, ideas, projects, and relationships. 96 pp.   Order No. 5470

Green Spirituality
Reflections on Belonging to a World Beyond Myself
  by Veronica Ray
  When you wonder, "What am I becoming spiritual for?" read *Green Spirituality*. Veronica Ray's meditations place special emphasis on moving beyond personal growth. This beautiful book is about caring for the human community—considering "Myself and Others," "Myself and Community," and "Myself and the Earth." 128 pp.   Order No. 5184

For price and order information, or a free catalog, please call our Telephone Representatives.

HAZELDEN EDUCATIONAL MATERIALS

1-800-328-9000   **1-612-257-4010**   **1-612-257-1331**
(Toll Free. U.S., Canada,   (Outside the U.S.   (FAX)
and the Virgin Islands)   and Canada)

Pleasant Valley Road • P.O. Box 176 • Center City, MN 55012-0176

Hazelden Europe • P.O. Box 616• Cork, Ireland
Telephone: Int'l Code+353+21+314318
FAX: Int'l Code+353+21+961269